A FIELD GUIDE TO NATURE MEDITATION

52 MINDFULNESS PRACTICES FOR JOY, WISDOM AND WONDER

MARK COLEMAN

To the earth and all her miraculous expressions of life.

And to all those who dedicate their lives to understanding and protecting the natural world.

PRAISE FOR MARK COLEMAN

"A Field Guide to Nature Meditation inspires us to get away from our screens, get outside and experience our beautiful, impermanent, living & dying world—a refuge that soothes our mind, strengthens our heart, and helps us remember our interconnection with all of life."

— TARA BRACH, AUTHOR OF *RADICAL ACCEPTANCE* AND *TRUSTING THE GOLD*

"A marvelous book, so rich with the spirit of practice and the soul of nature."

— ROSHI JOAN HALIFAX, ABBOT, UPAYA ZEN CENTER

"Coleman's book prompts readers to lean into the mysteriousness of life, to evoke curiosity, to feel into the awe that nature bestows, and to accept the gift of living existence. Both a meditation guide and a call-to-action to 'complete the cycle of love,' we are reminded to offer our love back to our planet, for the generosity and wisdom that it has shown us unconditionally."

— SHARON SALZBERG, AUTHOR OF
LOVINGKINDNESS AND *REAL CHANGE*

"Mark Coleman offers you beautiful ways to attend to life and mystery. If you do the practices here, they will open your heart, sensitize your awareness, connect you with all that breathes and lives, and revitalize your spirit."

— JACK KORNFIELD, AUTHOR OF *A PATH WITH
HEART*

"We spend so much of our time oblivious to the terrain breathing all around us. Distracted by the dazzle of the digital screen, caught up in worries and cravings, we are so often absent and elsewhere, out to lunch with relation to the present moment. Mark Coleman's field guide is the real deal, a lucid compendium of practices for the craft of awakening—simple skills for opening awareness, through the whole of one's body, to the animate earth in all its many-voiced wonder and strangeness."

— DAVID ABRAM, AUTHOR OF *BECOMING
ANIMAL,* AND *THE SPELL OF THE SENSUOUS*

"Most of what ails the world today is rooted in our alienation.

Beautifully written, this simple yet profound book will bring you back to our true home in nature. From its

author's calm and kind heart, the gentle, powerful practices in it offer many wonderful ways to enjoy and learn
from the natural world. This is an effective guide for
anyone looking for more delight, more awe, and greater
inner peace."

— RICK HANSON, PH.D., AUTHOR OF *RESILIENT:*
HOW TO GROW AN UNSHAKABLE CORE OF CALM,
STRENGTH, AND HAPPINESS

"A Field Guide to Nature Meditation is a wonderful book.
Drawing on a decades-long experience of meditation in a
wide variety of natural settings, Mark Coleman invites us
to join him in this joyous exploration of nature's beauty
and wisdom. From the simplest feeling of a gentle breeze
to the great mysteries of life and death, Mark guides us
into an ever-deepening appreciation and understanding of
the world around us. He is a rare example of someone
who has integrated the depth of his meditation practices
with the sensitivity of a naturalist marveling at what is
always right before us. A jewel of a book, and highly
recommended."

— JOSEPH GOLDSTEIN, AUTHOR
OF *MINDFULNESS: A PRACTICAL GUIDE TO*
AWAKENING

"For those called to let 'the more than human world' be
their meditation teacher, this book is your guide. Let it
open doorways of awareness your ancestors knew, and
you are remembering. A beautifully written, comprehen-
sive, and timely guide for this moment on Earth."

"I delighted in reading Mark Coleman's *A Field Guide To Nature Meditation,* which offers our senses 52 rich portals for experiencing our interconnected wholeness with the natural world around us. Mark offers us a seminal work of simple and elegant meditations that can be integrated into our daily lives for all who wish to embrace a natural path for awakening deeply and intimately to who they truly are."

CONTENTS

INTRODUCTION

NATURAL MINDFULNESS OUTDOORS

As I step outside of the isolated cottage in the woods at dawn, I leave behind the familiar and muted experience of being indoors. I move into the crisp morning air and feel a jolt of alertness as I sense the cold against my face. My attention quickens as I step barefoot on the spongy ground carpeted in pine needles. I realize how soft the forest floor is.

Suddenly I'm attuned to innumerable things I was oblivious of indoors. I'm acutely aware of all the faint sounds—whispers of the forest beginning to wake up and birds beginning their morning conversations. I recognize the subtle fragrance of the earth after the evening rain has moistened the soil. I begin to see infinite shades of green as light enters the forest canopy.

When I come across a small pond, I pause a while. The stillness of the water naturally draws me into a state of contemplation. I sense the quietude of the morning, the hush of the forest, the tranquility of stones that line the waters edge. I feel invited into a natural meditation, attuned to the serenity of nature. I notice the same peacefulness arising within me. The notion of being a visitor in the forest vanishes as I begin to feel part of the forest, welcomed and connected.

This, I remember, is why I step outdoors as often as possible, to experience the beauty, serenity and joy of nature. It allows me to access a natural quality of meditation, a state I call "meditative awareness," where one is naturally attentive. It is a quality that is fully embodied, meaning I am inhabiting my physical experience, attuned to my senses, grounded and alert.

This is mindfulness in nature and it is at the heart of Nature Meditation. It is a quality of attention we can cultivate in any natural landscape. And with the right intention, it is accessible anytime we spend time outdoors.

This book is a guide on how to develop this innate quality of mindfulness and how to bring this receptive mode of attention to a wide variety of experience in nature. Doing so is a path for joy, beauty and wonder. Be prepared to be surprised, to have your body energized, to have your heart opened to love and your mind touched by wonder and illumination.

WHY I'M WRITING THIS BOOK

I have had the delight and good fortune of leading mindfulness in nature programs for twenty years. For a similar length of time, I have also been leading mindfulness retreats in retreat centers. And while both are transformative for participants, I have always been struck by the contrast between what people experience on retreat in these two different locations.

Attendees on a nature retreat generally report feeling much more joy, peace, awe and wonder than when meditating indoors. They report how much easier it is to be mindful and how supportive nature is for maintaining awareness. They also report feeling a profound sense of connection with the natural world around them. I see how deeply their hearts open to love, to a deep appreciation of nature and all of the creatures within it.

Participants share how insights about themselves and the deeper truths of life come quite effortlessly in nature. They begin to see the preciousness and fragility of life in the natural world and how this awareness kindles a desire to protect the earth and become better stewards.

Once I began to see these differences, I began to write more about the subject, culminating in my first book, *Awake in the Wild*. I also started to focus more on leading meditation in nature programs and retreats worldwide. Ultimately, this led to offering Nature Meditation teacher trainings to support others doing this work.

It is for these reasons that I'm sharing this new work, to offer a variety of simple, portable and accessible practices that anyone can do in the outdoors, regardless of background, religious affiliation or meditation experience. So I welcome you in this journey and look forward to walking this Nature Meditation path together.

NATURE MEDITATION ANYWHERE

Some of you reading this may be wondering whether meditation is really something you can do. Perhaps you've tried to focus your attention and have seen it is not so easy. You may have discovered how much your mind thinks, how easily distracted you are, or how challenging it is to sustain focus. However, Nature Meditation is something anyone can do.

If you are reading this book there are probably many ways you already bring a meditative spirit to your time outdoors. By simply walking along a sandy beach, or gazing at a sunset, or swimming in a cool mountain lake you are, to some degree, learning to pay attention.

To meditate in nature is to bring an attentiveness to the world around you and a curiosity about your inner and outer environment. To do so means to draw on the innate quality of mindfulness, which is the simple capacity to be aware, to know what is happening in your direct experience.

This is possible for all of us. The reason for this guide to Nature Meditation is to show the numerous ways to cultivate this beautiful quality of attention. It is as simple as listening to the exquisite morning song of birds, or gazing at the infinite expanse of the night sky, or walking quietly through a forest, simply noticing what's happening around you.

The beauty of Nature Meditation is that it can be done anywhere, anytime you are outdoors. It can also be done sitting by a window or an open doorway at home, or even with a plant on your desk. Being mindful in nature can happen while sitting still on a park bench in the city, walking down a country lane, lying in a grassy meadow, listening to the pounding sound of waves, or hiking vigorously up a mountain. It can be practiced at sunrise or while gazing at the luminous night sky. Every situation in nature provides a rich opportunity to be present and to discover the wonders therein.

HOW TO USE THIS BOOK

Think of this book as a field guide to help you navigate all the different terrains and experiences you will encounter as you cultivate mindfulness outdoors. Since there are 52 meditations, you can select one practice to do each week of the year.

Some meditations are seasonal and some can be cultivated any time, any place. If you are new to meditation, I would suggest starting with the Meditation Fundamentals section as a way to become familiar with the basic principles of meditation and then expand out from there.

If you are an experienced meditator, feel free to select whatever meditation draws you, or what practice feels relevant to where you are outdoors or to what may be happening in your life. This guide contains a variety of practices—there are meditations that draw out your curiosity, ones that will touch your heart and others that bring a deepening intimacy with place. Certain practices will refine your sensory awareness, some will deepen attunement to the natural world and others will help foster profound insights and understanding.

This book is portable (as is the audio version). Take it with you as you go on hikes, head to the beach, retreat in the forest or sit in a city park. Once you have found a suitable place to meditate, find a comfortable posture, read through the meditation instructions and begin your practice. You can review the instructions at any time. You can also listen to the meditations on audio and be guided as you sit and practice

Whatever meditation you choose to do, please enjoy them and take them with you everywhere. These tools and techniques can serve you for the rest of your life!

DIGITAL DEVICES & BEING IN NATURE

Our lives now are very intertwined with technology. Even when we go into nature, we may be using our phone as a GPS or a camera, or to record sounds. We might use it to take notes as we reflect, or check the weather or a tide chart. However, research reveals that when we use our phones while in nature, this use of technology can dramatically impact our experience and erode the positive benefits of being outside. Our attention becomes narrowed and we inevitably get pulled into a digital world far removed from the aliveness of sensory experience around us.

Ironically, some of you will be reading this on a kindle or tablet or listening on your phone (that's okay!). We can use our digital devices skillfully. We just need to be careful to not let our attention be consumed by our device. Instead, we can use them minimally and have most, or all of our attention on our senses and on the natural environment around us.

On that note, I would also suggest letting go of taking photos when you are doing these practices. Simply enjoy the immediate visual experience rather than trying to capture it on your camera. Allow yourself to be as fully in the moment as you can, unmediated by technology. This will significantly deepen and improve your connection to the sensory world of nature.

MEDITATION
FUNDAMENTALS

TYPES OF MEDITATION

Throughout this book there are many ways to meditate. Most commonly they fall into these main categories: Sitting, Walking, Standing, Lying and Meandering meditations. They are primarily mindfulness-based sensory awareness practices, though some have more of an explicit heartfelt orientation. Given that many of them are done in the sitting posture, here are some important tips to sit comfortably.

SITTING MEDITATION POSTURE

Sitting outdoors is usually a bit more uncomfortable than in the coziness of our homes on a couch or in an armchair. However, there are many things you can do to sit with ease and uprightness outdoors.

Most importantly, you will want to support your lower back, so sitting on something that gives you a little height will help a lot. Ideally, you'll have your hips higher than your knees or feet. Sitting in this way helps bring more ease to the legs, knees and feet.

There are some simple items you can use to help your posture be more comfortable, which allow you to sit with relative ease and stillness for at least 20 minutes. The main options are:

1. Meditation cushion, sometimes called a zafu. This is often round, about 4-6 inches high, and allows you to sit off the ground. It's particularly useful if you like to meditate with crossed legs in front of you. If you plan to hike, there are inflatable cushions/zafus for easy transport or you could use a lightweight yoga block.
2. Meditation bench. This is my preferred option. Usually 6-8 inches high, these allow you to put your lower legs under you without strain and they are easier on the hips and are a great support for the lower back.
3. Back jack. These are L-shaped chairs that are foldable, lightweight and hence portable. Back jacks allow you to sit on the ground while providing some lower back support.
4. Nature. The natural world provides many good supports for sitting, like fallen tree trunks, large rocks or boulders. There are spaces that allow you to sit facing downwards, like a sloping hill, or rest your back up against, like a tree or rock face.
5. Chair. A lightweight, foldable chair that is portable is also a great option.

WHERE TO MEDITATE OUTDOORS

Fortunately, you don't need to hike to the top of Mt. Kilimanjaro or be in a remote canyon in the desert to successfully do these practices. Nature is everywhere and so meditation in nature can be done anywhere. It can be done sitting in your garden, walking in a city park, lying down in a meadow, or even beside an open window in your home or while gazing at a plant.

However, the more natural the setting—the further away you are from roads, buildings and the hustle and bustle of activity—the more potent the experience of nature can be. So if you can find a spacious park, a quiet beach, a simple woodland, or can walk up a hill or mountainside with a vista, then you will be more able to immerse your attention into the natural world.

Ideally you will have something to sit on, like the items previously noted, or find a place in nature that supports your seated posture (the chapter on Sit-Spot will give you more ideas on where to sit). It's important to feel comfortable. If it's hot, be sure to sit in the shade or wear a sun hat. If it is cold, wrap up well by bringing warm layers, like a hat, a scarf or perhaps a blanket to cover your legs. And remember to hydrate, especially in warmer climates.

HOW LONG TO MEDITATE

The meditations in this book can be done in as short as ten minutes and be extended comfortably to twenty or thirty minutes. You could take even longer, if you'd like, doing the meandering and walking practices.

SO WHAT IS MINDFULNESS?

The foundation of Nature Meditation practice is rooted in the timeless practice of mindfulness. Mindfulness is simply being aware. It is our innate capacity to pay attention in the present moment to our inner and outer experience. The fact that you are reading this is a simple act of mindfulness, attending to the written word on the page. And when you notice your mind drifts and gets distracted, that recognition is equally a mindful moment!

Mindfulness is both a quality of mind and a practice that anyone can develop systematically. Meditation is one of the most direct and potent ways to cultivate mindfulness through learning to train the attention. Developed in the Buddhist tradition for millennia, mindfulness has been successfully practiced globally by millions of people worldwide. It is particularly helpful today given how much our attention is scattered and pulled in many directions, especially to our digital screens and through multi-tasking.

For the past two decades, mindfulness has been the subject of thousands of research studies. It has been proven to improve mental clarity, well-being, mood, anxiety, sleep and many other conditions. And, perhaps most significantly, it has been proven to improve our capacity to focus and pay attention, something that is increasingly being eroded by our digital devices, our online habits and our consistent multi-tasking.

In the Buddhist tradition, mindfulness has been developed as a path of awakening, as a way to understand ourselves, to train the mind and to wake up to the nature of reality. Mindfulness can be the doorway to living with awareness, peace and freedom. It is available to us all. And it takes practice!

Generally, mindfulness is associated with meditating indoors, in a quiet room or meditation hall, focusing on one's breath, body sensations or on one's mind. When practiced indoors, meditation can feel like a struggle for many people, as the flood of thoughts easily overwhelms our noble efforts to focus. Being indoors amplifies the volume of our mind as there is little else to compete for attention.

However, in this book I offer a variety of ways and methods for cultivating the beautiful, simple and life-changing quality of mindfulness within nature's rich land-scapes and sensory stimuli. To cultivate mindfulness while sitting or walking outside means there is a rich tapestry of experience to attend to, to draw us into the aliveness of the present moment.

When we meditate outdoors, where sensory experience is vivid, alive and fluid, then it makes paying attention easier, less effortful and infinitely more enjoyable. This is one of the great benefits of Nature Meditation as it makes the practice of mindfulness more accessible and, at times, joyous and delightful!

In this book we will explore how to cultivate this jewel of mindfulness in many postures, from sitting and lying down to walking and meandering. As nature draws us into the present, we can quickly see how awareness—this natural knowing quality of mind—is innate and can be accessed anywhere. We will deepen our Nature Meditation practice and see how it is possible to live with meditative awareness, that every moment offers an opportunity to be mindful and aware.

THE 52 MEDITATIONS

PART ONE
ARRIVING PRACTICES

CHAPTER ONE
ARRIVING PRACTICE

Everything in nature invites us constantly to be what we are.

— GRETEL EHRLICH

Arriving in a particular place, mindfully aware and attuned, is one of the simplest and yet most important ways to enter into relationship with nature. It is a way of sensitively orienting to the environment you find yourself in. It allows us to let go of our busy, thinking mind and mental preoccupations and instead arrive in our senses in the moment.

On my Awake in the Wild nature programs, when I bring people to a particular place to meditate—perhaps in a forest, along an ocean bluff, or in a sandy canyon in the desert—I share this process of "arriving" as a way to begin to help people orient to the particularities of place.

Once you arrive at a place outdoors that you would like to spend time or meditate in, find somewhere you can sit or rest comfortably for ten to fifteen minutes. Prior to meditating or trying to be mindful, invite a quality of relaxation and rest at ease sitting on the earth.

Then open up your senses fully to begin the process of "arriving." Notice what immediately allures your attention. Look around and take in the variety of life here. You may be pulled to the array of colors around you, or to gaze at the tree canopy or at the clouds. Perhaps the intimacy with life on the ground catches your attention.

Notice the sounds of this place, the soundscape of the forest, the insects, frogs, or birdsong. You may notice the ebb and flow of sounds, particularly as winds blow through the landscape. Maybe you are captivated by the sound of silence and how that touches a sense of stillness within you.

Sometimes you may simply feel all the sensory impressions as you sit in this landscape—the softness or hardness of the ground, the breeze blowing against your skin, the warmth or coolness of the air, the sunlight against your body.

Occasionally you may sense the fragrances that are here, perhaps the rich smells of the forest after rainfall or the sweet aroma of blossoming flowers in Spring. Or you might notice the salty air with each inhale as you sit by the ocean.

One of the things that can captivate our attention is the dynamism of a place. You may be drawn to the movement of leaves in the trees, the changing patterns on the surface of water, the cumulus clouds mushrooming in the sky, or the way dappled light moves through the forest.

What is key to all these sense impressions is to notice how effortlessly you are brought into the present moment without any effort or strain. Nature spontaneously allures our curiosity to its effervescent, rich, changing forms.

This natural quality of knowing brings forth an important point—that being outside allows a more relaxed, natural quality of attention. Mindfulness practice outdoors, when attuned to our sensory experience, can be effortless and easeful and happens almost by itself.

So as you continue to sit here in this place, let your attention continue to be drawn to whatever catches your interest. See how easy it is to reside in the present moment. Observe how this simple act of arriving allows you to enter into a particular landscape, to become familiar with it. Notice how it deepens your sense of connection with life around you.

Each time you move to a different place outdoors, be sure to begin by doing this practice of "arriving" even if only for a few moments. Doing so will help you attune more intimately with wherever you are.

CHAPTER TWO

ASKING PERMISSION

Let us permit nature to have her way. She understands her business better than we do.

— MICHEL DE MONTAIGNE

Wisdom from indigenous traditions around the world provides profound wisdom in how to understand and live in harmony with the natural world. By contrast, the modern, materialist perspective has historically viewed nature as simply a resource in a mechanistic universe that humans can exploit for maximum production.

However, this simple practice of asking permission that I have learned from indigenous teachers in North America comes from the understanding that every single part of the natural world is animate, it is alive with presence and with spirit. So when we go into nature, we are entering a home, the abode of innumerable beings, a place that is filled with life and sentience.

When we go to someone's house, we enter only when we have been invited, when we have been given permission to enter. We step over the threshold aware that we are going into someone's space, and so we enter respectfully, with care.

So too when we go outdoors to a place to meditate, it behooves us to be mindful that we are entering the home of many beings, many life forms. And so, in the spirit of respect, it is a lovely practice to begin by asking permission to enter this natural place.

You may do this by being very specific, perhaps asking a particular grove of trees, or the animals of the woodland, or the birds in the canopy if you have permission to enter. You may ask it of the ground you walk on, of the hills, the mountains or the valley. Or, you can simply offer this request to all of the life forms in a place, asking if it is okay for you to enter and practice there.

You may hear or feel or sense a response. Or you may not. However, what is most important is the act of asking for permission. It shows that we are entering humbly, respectfully. It serves to remind us that we are always entering into a relationship when we step outdoors. It is not a one-way street of us having an experience. It is a two-way process of entering into a participatory experience with every living thing around us.

So, when you do go into any natural landscape, remember to do so with respect, reverence and care. Attune to the fact that you are entering the abode of countless life forms that know this land, this space as their home. This may open you up to a whole new way of relating to nature. This practice is also supported by the upcoming meditation on Being Known.

CHAPTER THREE

CULTIVATING A NATURE SIT-SPOT

Nature is not a place to visit. It is home.

— GARY SNYDER

There is a lovely tradition of people going into the outdoors, into a natural setting to what is known as a "sit-spot" or what I like to call a "favorite place" outdoors. The idea is you go to the same place every day, or at least every week, and spend time there with awareness, receptivity and curiosity.

The regularity of that immersive time in nature begins to open up a sensitivity to place. It allows an intimate attunement to how that particular environment changes with the cycles of seasons, during varieties of weather, during shifts in light and shadow, and at dawn and dusk.

One can get to know the changing migrations of birds over time and where particular birds like to nest, feed and sing. You can start to know the various animals that walk through this landscape and begin to see where they graze and rest. You can discover the insects that live their brief lives here. And you may come to understand a whole host of things that remain elusive to the fleeting visitor.

Many of the following meditations can be done whilst visiting your sit-spot so you get to bring a multi-dimensional awareness to a particular place. And of course the meditations can be practiced anywhere, each time in a different place if that is of interest. Coming here during each season you can get the sense of cycles, of how each place on the earth regenerates and moves through periods of decay and growth, of fallowness and abundance.

The main practice to do while in your sit-spot is to deepen your sensory awareness of being there. It can be helpful to begin with the arriving meditation previously described in Chapter 1. Then, after you have "arrived," continue to open your senses and attune to whatever draws you in the environment.

On certain days you may practice a listening meditation, where you simply close your eyes and listen to the soundscape at different seasons. At other times, you may lie down on the earth and gaze at the canopy from the ground. In other sessions, you may meander around this area touching the bark of trees, smelling the fragrant plants. Or you may walk and track for footprints of animals that move about at night.

It can be helpful to keep a journal of the various things you encounter over time, and the kinds of plants, leaves, animals, birds, and insects that change from season to season. As you deepen into a sense of place and intimacy with this landscape, notice how your sensitivity grows as you become more familiar. Over time it will be like visiting an old friend!

CHAPTER FOUR
KNOWING & BEING KNOWN

We still do not know one thousandth of one percent of what nature has revealed to us.

— ALBERT EINSTEIN

Generally, when we go outdoors into the natural world we have the sense that "I" am going to visit somewhere, explore something, have some experience that will happen to "me."

We tend to think of that process as a one-way phenomenon, as if we are the only one having the experience. In a conversation we may say: "'I' am going to walk through the forest" or "'I' am off to hike the mountain."

Similarly, we may share how we love gazing at ocean tide-pools, getting close to flowers to smell their fragrance, or walking barefoot in the park to feel wet grass underfoot. In that framing, there is an implicit assumption that we are the only ones having an experience.

What would it be like to understand that we are always

in a relationship with the natural world, which simultaneously is in intimate contact with us? Can we realize how experience in nature is always a two-way process? The natural world is just as much, if not more aware of us as we are conscious of it. There is a simultaneous dance of knowing and being known.

Once we realize we are part of any landscape we enter into, then we can be aware not just of the life around us, but how we too are being known, seen, felt, heard, and sensed by myriad life forms around us.

For instance, birds will often change their song as humans enter their territory. Crows and ravens may get curious, eyeing you from the canopy and sharing a conversation about what they see. Snakes shift away into longer grass as they feel the vibration of our steps. Insects may be drawn to you (as food) or repelled by your presence as danger.

Similarly, animals like coyote, bear, cougar and fox may sniff your scent and know to keep their distance. Deer hear us from far away and stay deep in the trees. So too trees and plants may have some inkling of your presence as you walk on their roots, lean against their trunks or pluck their flowers.

In this meditation, begin by going outdoors. It could be simply walking into your garden or out to a local park, venturing deep into a forest, sitting by a particular tree, or going any other place where you can connect intimately with the natural world around you.

Begin this practice by sitting down on the earth. Take some moments to open up your senses. Look around you and notice all the life forms you behold with your eyes. Then, by simply listening, absorb all the sounds around you. As you inhale, notice the smells and fragrance from this landscape. Feel the sensations of sitting on the earth, observing the particular quality of hardness of the ground or softness of sand or grass.

Now shift your attention to all the ways that the life in this particular landscape is similarly knowing you, sensing your presence. What creatures may be seeing you, perhaps even unseen by you? What creatures in the soil or underground are sensing your footsteps? What beings may be aware of your particular smell? What beings can hear the sounds you make?

Are there animals or grasses that are tracking your footsteps? Are the trees perhaps aware of your presence as you lean against them? What species are aware of your presence, since by simply showing up there, you influence and change the living landscape as you become momentarily part of that place.

As you open up your senses and become aware in this way, notice not just what is around you, but also how it is to sense being known, felt and seen. Notice if that makes you feel more part of a living landscape, not just a human having an experience, but a living part of the earth that is being experienced by many life forms.

PART TWO
ESTABLISHING MINDFULNESS FOUNDATIONS

CHAPTER FIVE

BREATHING WITH NATURE

Every breath we take, every step we make, can be filled with peace, joy and serenity.

— THICH NHAT HANH

Modern life tends to accentuate a sense of feeling separate. We mostly live inside, cut off from the elements and the vibrancy of life outdoors. We live much of our lives looking at screens rather than at people. Living so separately can create a sense of anxiety and alienation.

In contrast, when we go outdoors we immediately feel how interconnected everything is, including ourselves. This meditation is an exploration of this interconnected awareness through the simple act of breathing. When we feel more connected, we tend to feel more alive and more supported in life.

Begin this simple meditation by finding a comfortable posture outdoors. Ideally, you will be sitting near trees, or by a meadow, grasses, or plants. As you find your seat, spend a moment gazing at the flora around you. Notice the trees, grasses, and plants both near and far.

Reflect on how flora are engaged in the wondrous process of photosynthesis, soaking up light from the sun, transforming it into energy, and drawing carbon in through their leaves and releasing oxygen. Reflect on the miracle of how plant life thrives in this way, creating an atmosphere rich in life-giving oxygen.

Now close your eyes or lower your gaze and turn your attention to your inner environment. As you sense yourself on the earth, notice your body is breathing by itself. Start to feel the rhythmic wave-like motion of breath. Feel the gentle stream of cool air enter the nose, tickling the throat. Notice how the inhale expands the chest, rib-cage, shoulders and upper back. Feel the motion of the diaphragm and belly moving in and out.

Without trying to change or manipulate the breath, attune to all the different sensations. Notice the stillness between breaths and see if that echoes the stillness around you.

If your attention wanders into thinking, acknowledge that and then release the thought and orient awareness again to breathing. No need to judge the thought. Thinking is a process of nature. Our practice is to recognize being lost in thought and then return attention to the breath over and over again.

Similarly, when your attention is drawn to other things like sounds, feelings or other phenomena, acknowledge those experiences and then re-establish awareness of breath. In this way, we are training the attention to focus and steady by attuning to one experience.

As awareness of breath deepens, turn your attention to

the inhale. As you breathe in, be mindful that you are taking in oxygen released from the leaves, plants and grasses. If you are by the ocean, bear in mind the air is pervaded with oxygen released from phytoplankton—their exhale is literally what keeps us alive.

We are connected with forests, grasslands and plants in invisible ways through the medium of air. Notice what happens when you breathe and reflect in this way. You are literally breathing with trillions of trees each and every moment.

In the same way, sense your exhale. As your body breathes out, you release carbon into the atmosphere. That CO_2 is absorbed by the plant kingdom. As you breathe, sense this reciprocal relationship. You are breathing with forests and plants who depend on that carbon dioxide.

Continue to attune to breath sensations as if it was the first time you've breathed. Take in this simple miracle with a curious attention. Be aware that each breath connects you to the vastness of life around you. Each breath is shared with all living, breathing animals, birds, insects and marine species. Continue this practice as long as feels comfortable. That may be as short as five to ten minutes or up to thirty minutes or longer.

As you bring this meditation to a close, observe how being mindful of breath in this way feels. How has it affected your body? What happens in your heart and mind as you are aware of breathing with all photosynthesizing life?

Practice awareness of breath throughout the day. Your breath can be your best friend when it comes to training attention and learning to be mindful, embodied and present.

CHAPTER SIX
GROUNDING WITH EARTH

Heaven is under our feet as well as over our heads.

— HENRY DAVID THOREAU

L iving indoors, we are most of the time cut off from feeling our connection to the earth under us, from the richness of grasses, soil and rock. Looking at screens all day we can easily forget we are part of the earth's moving surface. When we are separated in that way we can feel ungrounded and uncentered in ourselves. This meditation is an antidote to this and allows for a sense of grounding through the immediacy of connection with earth.

Begin this meditation by finding a comfortable place outdoors. This could be in your garden, in a park or wood-land, or in a meadow. Wherever it is, make sure there is somewhere to sit steadily and with ease on the ground. It is easier to maintain an upright posture if you sit on a downward facing slope. If the ground is wet or cold, put something down that suitably protects you.

As you take your seat, spend a moment gazing at all the expressions of earth around you. Take in the trees, rocks, grasses, plants and soil. Sense how they all come from earth and are expressions of the earth.

Then close your eyes or lower your gaze. Turn your attention inward. Observe how the landscape of your body feels as you take your seat on the ground. Sense all the ways your body is in contact with the earth below you. Feel the intimacy of that connection through the sensations of touch in your feet, calves, thighs, buttocks and skin.

Notice how the earth is always there, steady, strong and abiding. Its presence is forever available. Sense how it actually supports you physically, providing steady ground wherever you are. How does it feel to sense that support under your bones?

As you tune into the earth, sense it's vastness spreading out below you in infinite directions. As part of the earth, you too are not separate from that immensity. Does anything arise within you when you open awareness to sense that immensity?

Now imagine you are like a tree, that you also have roots going deep into the earth, moving though topsoil, down into crevices and cracks in the stone. Sense how you too are rooted to the earth and can draw on that steady, grounded quality in the ways trees can.

As you continue sitting, each time your attention is drawn elsewhere, notice that and bring awareness back to the solid connection with the earth underneath you. Allow your body to rest into the supportive quality of the ground. Feel how, like a tree, you can be rooted and steady, yet at the same time supple and flexible. You can sit in stillness without the need to be stiff.

Sit in this posture as long as you like, anywhere from ten minutes to half an hour and repeatedly return your focus to sensing the rooted quality of earth. As you end the practice, sense in your body how you can carry that grounded quality with you wherever you go.

CHAPTER SEVEN

EXPLORING THE BODY AS A DOORWAY TO SENSORY CONNECTION

Just being surrounded by bountiful nature, rejuvenates and inspires us.

— E.O. WILSON

We are sensory creatures. Our ancestors lived in intimate connection with the elements and had an attunement to their senses and the sensory world of nature around them. Even though we have lost much of that sensitivity, whenever we go outdoors our body naturally reawakens to a whole field of sensory experience that is alive, dynamic and connected.

In this practice, you will explore how the body is an amazing portal for connecting with the sensory world in nature. In doing so, you will see how this reveals the aliveness of our physical experience and our innate embeddedness with life.

In this meditation, sit anywhere outdoors that is comfortable, ideally where you are open to a range of sensory experiences around you. First, feel all the ways your body is in touch with the ground. Sense what this particular part of the earth feels like, as each place on the earth has its own quality, energy and ambience. Observe any quality of stillness, steadiness or stability, either in the earth or in yourself.

Continue to feel that visceral connection with the ground as you expand your range of focus to include the whole field of sensations in your body. What other ways do you experience contact with the natural world around you? Be aware of the sensations on your skin as the breeze kisses your face or moves your hair. Feel the wind viscerally as its force moves over your body.

Notice how sounds can also be felt physically as you hear the sound of a raven cry or the wind roar in the leaves or whistle through the pines.

Now shift your attention to breathing. As you inhale, be curious about the quality of air. Notice if there is a fragrance, a particular smell perhaps from the trees, soil, or flowers around you. Be curious if the air is moist or dry. Notice whether it feels cool and crisp or warm and soft. Be mindful of tickling sensations as cool air enters the nostrils and throat and warm air is exhaled from the body.

As the bellows of your lungs expand, feel the sense of invigoration as you inhale. Notice the quality of release as you exhale. Be mindful how, with each breath, you are connecting with the inhale and exhale of leaves, plants and grasses. What happens when you attune to that intimate connection?

Similarly notice the range of temperature and how the body is exquisitely attuned and adjusting to the most subtle shifts in warmth and coolness. Sense warm sunlight as it touches your skin. Open to sensations of cold as it tingles your face or pierces deep into your body. Try to stay receptive to either experience.

As you continue sitting, bring awareness to the ongoing range of physical sensations. These can be felt as tingling, pulsing and vibration, piercing, rubbing, touching, or pressure. You may feel sensations of expansion, contraction, heaviness or lightness.

At times, notice pleasurable sensations like the warm sun on your body, the cool breeze on your skin or the sense of spaciousness around you. Notice how it feels to open to delicious sensory experiences in your body.

Continue to sit for fifteen to thirty minutes, observing this dynamism of the inner landscape of body sensations and how intimately they are connected to the outer environment, sensing how your body is a microcosm of the earth, with its valleys and peaks, terrains of warmth and coolness, having its beauty, challenges and range.

Upon completing the meditation, notice the influence of this practice. How do you feel in your body, heart and mind? Slowly open your eyes and take in the landscape around you, remembering as you move into your day to stay connected with the landscape of your body as a rich and complex expression of earth.

CHAPTER EIGHT
BEING WITH PAIN AND DISCOMFORT IN THE BODY

The intensity of the pain depends on the degree of resistance to the present moment.

— ECKHART TOLLE

Contrary to popular belief, as sublime as meditation can be, it is not always easy. We are often challenged by the busyness of the mind, the turbulent emotions or physical discomfort. In this practice we will explore how to work with some of the physical challenges as you meditate outdoors.

Begin by going outside and finding a place where you can sit with relative ease, like on a park bench, on a cushion on the ground, on a downward sloping hill, or on a soft, sandy beach. Close your eyes and notice all the sensations that arise that evoke a sense of both pleasure and ease as you sit on the earth.

Notice any quality of relaxation in the body. Be mindful of any enjoyment of the breeze, sunlight, warmth, sounds, smells or spaciousness around you. The more you can turn your attention to what is uplifting, the easier you can open to difficult or unpleasant experiences. This is known as "resourcing," attuning attention to what is nourishing.

When working with any difficulty, the breath can be a great resource, so open your attention to include breathing. Become intimate with changing sensations of breath and notice any pleasurable quality. Observe how attunement to breathing brings you swiftly into the present. You can return to breathing as a home base for attention during this practice.

Similarly, open awareness to the soundscape. Notice how listening to nature sounds can evoke spaciousness and connection to life around you. It can also bring delight and pleasure as you listen to the sound of rain, waves, birdsong or breeze.

Once you feel grounded in awareness of breathing and listening, observe any less pleasurable bodily sensations, like aches, tension, or areas of pain and intensity, perhaps in the knees, neck or lower back. Or simply be present to an area of strong sensation, like the sit bones touching the ground. Keep your attention there with a soft, kind attitude.

Try to open fully to this experience, feeling it, sensing all the nuances of it. It can be helpful to label or name it, which can bring more clarity and understanding. You could label it as "pain" or "tightness," "piercing," "pressure" or "tension." Notice how it is rarely one monolithic thing but a mass of changing sensations that ebb and flow.

Now observe your relationship to the discomfort. Can you meet it with acceptance or is there resistance, judgment, fear or contraction to it? Usually these kinds of reactions simply exacerbate the pain. If possible, try to soften any contraction or tightening around the tension. As hard as this can be, learning to be present in this way can grow your capacity to endure any experience.

With physical pain, it is kind and wise to move your body to a more comfortable posture when the discomfort is too much. You may also shift attention to a part of your body that feels more easeful, or attune to breath or listening as a way to bring ease. This is resourcing to both mind and body.

Continue to sit observing the inner landscape of bodily sensation for anywhere from ten to thirty minutes. Continue to oscillate attention between any discomfort in the body and an area that feels ease. If necessary, use sounds, breath or opening the eyes as a way to resource.

Your body is a microcosm of the earth, with its valleys and peaks, its terrains of beauty and challenge, pains and joys. Mindfulness practice is developing an attitude that is open to all of it.

When you end the meditation, notice the influence of sitting in this way. What impact does it have on your body, heart and mind to open to less pleasurable physical experience?

As you move into your day, stay connected with the terrain of your body and be open, curious and caring when bodily experience is challenging. This is a great metaphor and training for working with all adversity in life.

CHAPTER NINE

ABIDING IN SENSORY AWARENESS

I go to nature to be soothed and healed, and to have my senses put in order.

— JOHN BURROUGHS

One of the delights and strengths of Nature Meditation practice is how it opens us to the sensory dimension of experience. It supports an enlivening in the body as we wake up to our animal nature. It also attunes us to the sensory world with all its beauty and diversity.

In our lives there can be many challenging things we don't want to be present for, so we often check out. By opening our senses in nature, however, we can experience so much joy, pleasure, delight, wonder and awe. Why wouldn't we want to stay present in the beautiful natural landscapes we find there?

Begin this practice by going outdoors to a place rich in sensory experience, where you can listen to an interesting soundscape, see a variety of colors and flora, or where you can feel the movement of breeze, sun and shade, or sense the aliveness of the ocean or a stream.

Then, take your seat on the earth and close your eyes. Sense all that can be felt as your body is in contact with the earth. Notice the rich variety of touch as you feel the hardness, softness, ruggedness or smoothness of the land underneath you. Be present to how these sensations feel in your body and how they change.

Then open attention to include the range of physical sensations. Notice when the body feels invigorated and enlivened by the fresh air or cool breeze. Sense how your animal nature wakes up outdoors and becomes more attuned to a variety of stimuli and sense experiences.

Be mindful how the body is a portal to connect with the landscape around you. Feel the skin connected to the cool air. Observe how your face registers movement of wind and breeze. Notice how your body responds to the slightest temperature fluctuation, from the warmth of the sun to the coolness of shade.

Now include sensations of breathing. As you breathe, notice the various subtle and coarse smells that pervade the air. Smell the fragrant blossoms, the scent of animals, the rich odor of cut grass or the earthiness of the humus below you. Observe how fleeting and ephemeral but sometimes potent and evocative smells are.

Now open to the field of sounds. Being outside is a wonderful arena for listening to the soundscape of nature. Let your attention expand to the furthest sounds. Notice the symphony of sounds and at times focus on specific ones, like the call of a raven, the hum of insects, the sound of leaves rustling in the canopy or even silence.

Continue to meditate with this open sensory aware-ness, being present to whatever sense experience is most predominant. Let awareness move amongst the variety of sensations of the body in this environment, listening to sounds near and far, attuning to the air as you breathe, noticing fleeting smells and fragrances, sensing spacious-ness or groundedness, noticing the fluid movement of temperature, breeze and light.

Lastly, open the eyes and include the rich field of experi-ence of sight. Meditating with the eyes open means simply to allow the eyes to be receptive and open to all the visual impressions of color, form, shape, movement and texture. As you sit with eyes open, try to not lose touch with the other senses as you take in the richness and variety of the visual field.

Continue to meditate in this way to open to the whole panorama of sensory experience, moment by moment. Notice how it feels to be present to the richness of the sensory world. Let your attention move to whatever sense experience is most predominant in the moment. Observe how naturally your body and its senses can both be present to the life around you.

As you end this practice, continue to stay in touch with all of your senses as you move through your day, noticing how it can deeply enrich your lived experience.

PART THREE
ENGAGING WITH
MOVEMENT PRACTICES

CHAPTER TEN

MEANDERING MEDITATION

Traverse the world with ever-broadening scope of attention to reality, ever-widening circles of curiosity.

— MARIA POPOVA

There are many ways to mindfully explore the natural world. One method is through a variety of sitting meditations as we have explored earlier in this book. One of my favorite ways is through meandering, or what in England we may call "rambling" or "bimbling," meaning to walk at a leisurely pace.

Meandering is leisurely strolling through a landscape with full attentiveness. However, the key distinction from a typical walk is that with meandering we let the body guide the walking. We listen to what the body and its senses are drawn to. We let go of the typical goal-oriented focus and instead allow ourselves to be lured and drawn by curiosity to the natural world.

Begin by going outdoors where there is space to

wander, perhaps in a local park, forest, meadow or a beach. Once you find a suitable place, take a moment to pause and close your eyes or lower your gaze. Stand or sit still for a few minutes to arrive into the present moment as you sense your body and breath and notice how this particular landscape feels.

When you are ready, open your eyes and see what you are naturally drawn to. Listen to the body and let it lead. Maybe you are allured to stay standing where you are and feeling the warm sun on your face. Or maybe you are pulled into the shade to feel the cool air there.

Let your body walk slowly, mindfully, sensing your feet touching and caressing the earth. Perhaps there is a desire to go barefoot to feel the cool wet grasses or to sense the texture of sand or forest floor beneath you. With each step feel the intimacy of connection as your foot is met by the earth. What does that contact with the ground feel like?

Walk in whatever direction attracts you, which may be to walk in small circles or to a particular thing. As you walk, let your body be engaged with the environment. You may be drawn to a particular tree, to lean against its trunk or to stand nearby, or to touch and smell the cinnamon bark of a particular ponderosa pine.

Similarly, as you stroll you may feel the invitation to pause, to get down on your hands and knees and feel the morning dew on the grasses, or to bend closer to look at a tiny flower hiding in the undergrowth. Or perhaps a beetle or grasshopper catches your attention and you let yourself be present to that insect for a while.

Keep listening to where the body is drawn. After attending closely to something, you may be inclined to get up and meander again, perhaps this time into a clearing where you can gaze up at the vastness of the sky or into the canopy. Maybe you are enticed to a stand of trees where you can simply walk slowly among them.

At times you may feel the pull to smell a particular flower or blossom. If you are in a location where there are edible plants or fruit you may pause to taste and eat a particular offering of nature, savoring the rich flavors and aromas. Let yourself continue to be invited in this way.

Throughout the practice it is important to keep your attention in the physical sensory present. Be mindful not to be consumed in thinking about what you attend to. Simply be with the direct, immediate experience through the senses. And each time you become lost in thought, gently release those thoughts and orient back to meandering, sensing and enjoying the natural landscape.

And when nothing particular calls your attention, simply keep meandering, sensing your footsteps on the earth, your body moving through space, and the rich sensory environment around you. Let yourself walk like this for as long as you like, which may be as short as ten minutes but could be as long as a few hours or the whole day!

CHAPTER ELEVEN

MEANDERING WITH JOY & DELIGHT

Forget not that the earth delights to feel your bare feet and the winds long to play with your hair.

— KHALIL GIBRAN

In this meandering meditation we will engage in another walking practice, but this time oriented to the beautiful qualities of joy and delight in the natural world. This is a wonderful way to feel how nature uplifts the heart and brightens the mind.

When meditation has a particular intention—in this case to incline to joy—it doesn't mean that quality will necessarily be accessible. It means that we are creating the conditions for joy to arise. This can be true to develop any quality. It's called "inclining the mind."

When joy does arise, then, as the words of the English poet William Blake point to, we can "kiss the joy as it flies, and live in eternity's sunrise." The implication here is that we appreciate and enjoy when the heart is uplifted by delight, and let go when the sweetness of joy passes.

In this meditation, go outdoors to a place that you particularly appreciate and enjoy. It might be a coastal walk, an enchanting place in the woods, or in a beautiful garden or park.

Begin meandering—walking slowly and mindfully— with your senses attuned to your environment. Let yourself be drawn to whatever allures you. Be particularly oriented to anything that uplifts your spirits, that sparks delight, joy, appreciation, or simply brings a smile to your face.

You may be pulled to the myriad joys that can be had through the eyes. Perhaps you meander over to a bed of flowers to enjoy bees nuzzling into golden blossoms. Or you may be drawn to a clearing in the trees, to sense the rapture of an expansive vista. Or you find yourself gazing at a squirrel, deer or a bird that brings delight.

As you keep meandering, let yourself pause each time something in your visual field draws you in. Take at least 20-30 seconds to savor that particular experience. Feel the experience of joy in your body and heart, letting it saturate you.

Similarly, you may find that the sense of touch evokes a sense of delight as you feel the smooth texture of leaves, wet with dew. Or perhaps you are allured to a broad tree trunk to feel its crinkly, gnarled bark and that too evokes joy.

Let yourself be drawn into the enchantment of smell from nearby blossoms or fragrant herbs, from desert sage or other aromatic plants. Notice the sweet joy when we catch the smell of rose, lavender or jasmine or the odor of fresh cut grass.

Likewise turn your attention to the soundscape, to the symphony of sounds around you. Notice how the simple sound of a trickling stream, the rhythmic sounds of waves, or the innocent call of a bird can bring unexpected rapture and delight.

Keep meandering, letting yourself be drawn to whatever uplifts you, to any experience that brings a simple happiness or a smile. Pay attention to how the outer landscape of nature continues to touch the inner landscape of the heart and mind. Let yourself fully take in any uplifting emotions that are evoked. Be mindful of how joy feels in the body, noticing the expansive quality it brings.

Continue to meander as long as feels interesting. Remember you can incline your attention to joy in any moment, anywhere, even as you sit by a window indoors, gazing at the pink sky at dawn, listening to the morning song of birds, or watching the billowing cumulus clouds before a storm.

CHAPTER TWELVE

MEANDERING WITH BEAUTY

If you truly love nature, you will find beauty everywhere.

— VINCENT VAN GOGH

There is so much beauty on this earth, it is abundant everywhere. Nature gives us infinite possibilities to bathe in her beauty. Attuning to what is beautiful can be one of the more elevating human experiences. It simply requires us to pay attention, to slow down enough to let such richness touch us.

In this practice we will meander with beauty, which means to let yourself be drawn to whatever experience in nature you find alluring, graceful, elegant, exquisite or refined. Beauty, it has been said, is in the eye of the beholder. And so we may find anything and everything beautiful depending on the state of our mind and the quality of our perception.

Begin this meandering meditation by selecting a place

where you know there are many things that you find beautiful in a landscape. Perhaps it is among tide pools or amidst a wildflower meadow. It may be in a botanical garden or among an ancient grove of trees. Or it could simply be in your neighborhood where you appreciate the abundance of flora that spill out from people's gardens in springtime.

Begin by standing still and taking a few moments to establish mindfulness. Turn attention to your body, sensing your feet touching the ground. Take a few slow, mindful breaths, and then open your attention to all the sensory experience around you—sounds, smells, breeze, temperature, and all the sights and colors.

Now, begin your meandering, letting yourself be drawn by beauty. You could take one sense faculty at a time beginning with seeing. Walk around this landscape and notice whatever captivates your attention in the visual field. Let your gaze absorb into whatever enchants you and attune to the beauty within that experience.

In this practice you may only walk a short distance as you find yourself intoxicated by the beauty you find in just a particular plant, flower or pond. Or you may meander far, just letting beauty touch you lightly as you move through the terrain.

Often we notice beauty when we pay close attention. So give yourself some time to gaze at the exquisite patterns of veins in leaves, and the beautiful way light illuminates the leaf and its form. Attune to the perfect symmetry of flower petals that have their own quiet beauty. Notice the curvaceous forms of lichen on rocks or the brazen, bold forms of blossoms.

Similarly you may find beauty in the dazzling array of

color in nature. You might bathe in the copious shades of green in a forest or garden. Or you may be drawn into the lush colors of a garden, the deep gold of poppies, the crisp whites of jasmine petals or the rich velvet of a rose. As you do so, notice how that beauty touches you.

Sometimes you might be captured by the beauty of movement. Meandering along the shoreline you may be struck by the exquisite curve of a wave, or the way the ocean spray creates rainbows. Likewise, you may be trans-fixed by the beautiful patterns as waves drift in and out across the sand. Lifting your gaze to the sky, you may discover the beauty of billowing cumulus clouds, or the way the setting sun streaks a stunning crimson across the sky.

Continue to meander in this way, listening to what beauty draws your body and heart. Let yourself be surprised. Perhaps by gazing at a muddy pool, a simple stone, an old tree stump or a bleached white bone, you may find beauty in that simplicity.

In the same way, notice beauty through your other senses. Explore the exquisite fragrance of flowering blos-soms or the scent of fresh cut grass. Take in the rich smells of a forest after rainfall, or the evocative salty sea air.

Try touching the trunks of trees, the smooth skin of eucalyptus or the silky bough of a manzanita. Feel the smoothness of icicles or the delicacy of water in a stream.

Open to all the ways you are allured in a soundscape, like hearing morning bird song. We can find beauty listening to the symphony of cicadas singing at dusk or the silence of a desert landscape. The sound of silence, alas, has its own quiet beauty that touches the heart.

Whatever the source, keep inclining the attention to

beauty and notice how attuning in that way is a wonderful uplift for the heart and mind. Once you know how to do this, you can incline to beauty anywhere. And nature provides infinite possibilities for enjoying this quality.

CHAPTER THIRTEEN

MEANDERING WITH LOVE

Study nature, love nature, stay close to nature. It will never fail you.

— FRANK LLOYD WRIGHT

So many of us are drawn to nature by a deep, heartfelt connection. We are moved by the love we feel for the earth's beauty, her miraculous displays and her tender, vulnerable life forms. Given all this, it is a delightful practice to feel profound love when we are outdoors. This meditation is designed for just that.

Begin by going outdoors to one of your favorite places. It may be your regular sit-spot, or your garden or a place that touches your heart. As you arrive there, first let yourself pause, perhaps sitting or leaning against a tree or rock, and notice what you feel in this place.

Open your senses here and be mindful of what evokes the many facets of love in this environment. Perhaps it is care for the old trees, affection for the playful songbirds, or tenderness for the delicate flowers and grasses. Maybe it is a loving appreciation for an ancient rock or for the sounds of a tinkering stream. Let yourself attune to and bathe in these qualities. What quality of heart is evoked here?

Then begin to meander moving to what allures your heart. Sometimes you may be drawn to nature's tiny expressions. Perhaps your eye catches the tenacity in the smallest of flowers, the resoluteness of an iridescent beetle walking in the undergrowth, or a colony of ants moving busily on a mound. Notice how seeing life in these small ways can evoke a sense of care or love.

Continue to meander and see what else can be felt in the heart. Notice what happens when you attune to the vulnerability of life as you watch hawks preying on mice, lizards catching flies, crabs chasing other crabs, or an earthworm uprooted from the soil exposed to the predation of a bird. Feel the impact of these on your heart. You may feel a sense of protectiveness or compassion for the tenderness of the worm, or the hunger of the birds.

Similarly, as you meander notice your heart when you encounter an animal. Observe what happens when you see a young fawn lying in the grass, when encountering a squirrel staring down at you from a tree, or when you catch the movement of earth under a mole hill. Even seeing mice, snakes, skunks or other creatures that you may wish to avoid can equally evoke a sense of love and appreciation for all their uniqueness and their wish to survive.

If you meander in a very familiar place, like your garden or your favorite woodland, notice the relationship you may have with particular trees, species, plants or rocks. Sometimes familiar parts of a terrain can feel like old friends.

Sense if your heart feels a kinship, love or connection with aspects of the landscape here.

Along with feeling love for what you encounter while meandering, you may also wish to express your love. For example, you can express heartfelt qualities through words, wishes or a simple radiating love from your heart. You may silently wish a particular tree, lizard, bird or plant to be well, to be safe from harm, to be protected, to be well-nourished.

Notice what happens when you wish for the well-being of the life around you. Does it bring more connection? Do you feel more warmth, friendliness or love? You can also extend that same wish for the people you may pass by, who are also just part of nature.

Continue this meandering for as long as feels useful. You may find anywhere from twenty or thirty minutes to an hour is a good amount of time to sense your love for the natural world.

And of course you can continue to meander, sit or walk with this attunement to love throughout your day. Observe how, when you bring attention to the quality of love, it often becomes more available and can at times deepen your connection and appreciation of the natural world and all the beings within it.

CHAPTER FOURTEEN

HIKING WITH SENSORY AWARENESS

We live on the leash of our senses.

— DIANE ACKERMAN

Often, we walk or hike with a destination in mind and our attention can easily get lost in the goal. In doing so, we become less present to the natural world we are walking in. In this practice, the invitation is to take a hike and open attention to include all the senses as a way to connect with nature every step of the way.

Before setting out, pause for a moment and reflect on your intention for your walk. Is there a quality you would like to cultivate, like focus, relaxation or acceptance? Is there a facet of nature that you wish to pay attention to, like light, fauna or particular plants? Is there a specific sense experience, like hearing, smelling or breathing that you wish to orient towards? The more intentional you are on your hike, the more likely the aspiration will be realized.

Now, take some moments just to stand still and be

present to your body standing on the earth, feeling your feet solidly on *terra firma*. Notice the quality of your physical experience today.

As you stand, you may choose to do a "weather report" where you sense your body, heart and mind and select a word that describes how each of those inner terrains feels. This is an instant way of reading how you are.

Then begin your walk. As a way to orient to the present moment, rather being lost in your thoughts, keep your attention attuned to your footsteps. Feel each time your foot touches the ground and notice the quality and texture of the earth under you. Feel how the earth meets each step.

Then attend to the physicality of walking. Notice how, with each step, the body sways, muscles tense and relax, bones swing and move. Feel how the whole body coordinates movement and balance with each step. There is no need to look at your body or feet but simply sense the walking experience from within.

Once you have established mindful walking, begin to open up the field of attention. As you walk through the landscape, notice the changing temperatures. Feel how it fluctuates from cold shade to hot sun, from valley to peak, from the coolness of a stream to the warmth of the open air.

Be curious about subtle fragrances that perfume the landscape as you walk past flowers, blossoms, trees and streams. Notice how these ebb and flow depending on where you are, whether it's damp or dry, winter or summer.

Open awareness to the ever-changing soundscape. Observe how sounds ebb and flow depending on the topography. While walking by a stream, notice the way sound intensifies or diminishes depending on your proximity to the stream. Be mindful of birdsong and how your presence can change bird calls. Listen to the sounds of silence and its contrast with the roar of gusty winds or the gentle rustle of leaves.

As you continue to expand attention, be mindful of the visual field. Let the eyes open to the furthest vista. Take in the spaciousness of the sky. Notice the tiny life forms on the ground. Soak up the array of colors, the shades of green or blue. Gaze at the form of leaves, the arc of a bird's flight, the shapes of flowers, the symmetry of flowers blooming together.

Walk with an open, choiceless awareness. Let your attention move to whatever calls in the moment, whether that be a sound, sight, smell, taste or touch sensation. From time to time focus on a particular sense door, like hearing or smelling, and let that be the locus of your attention. Notice how each of these sense experiences impacts you.

As you walk, keep orienting to the rich sensory experience that is unfolding around you. Each time you notice your attention has drifted from the present or you have become lost in thinking, simply ask yourself what else is happening in this sensory moment and let the attention recalibrate to that.

Continue this walking meditation for as long as long as feels helpful. When you return from your hike, observe how you feel and perhaps do another three-point check-in to sense the difference from how you felt from the start to the end of the hike. Know that you can practice this sensory walking practice anywhere, anytime.

CHAPTER FIFTEEN

WALKING WITH ANIMAL SENSES

An animal's eyes have the power to speak a great language.

— MARTIN BUBER

Coyotes, hawks, whales and dragonflies are wonderful teachers of presence, attention and focus. They are masters at being aware and attuned to their environment. They have so much to teach us about being present in nature.

In this meditation, we will draw on the inspiration of many creatures for our walk. For example, we will walk stealthily like a fox, sniffing scents in the air. We will open up our vision with owl eyes, having a 360-degree view. We will listen acutely like a deer to the faintest of sounds. We will attune like a snake with its belly on the earth feeling touch and vibration.

Begin your walk by going out into a landscape, preferably away from people. As you walk, ideally barefoot, feel an intimate connection to the ground. Call to mind a wild cat, like a cougar, bobcat or lynx. Imagine your toes are like the soft pads of their feet, spreading quietly with each step. Walk as silently as possible, stepping first with your toes before placing your heel down.

Sense your wild cat nature, moving with stealth through the meadows and woodland. How would a cougar orient to this landscape? What would a bobcat be attuned to as she walks quietly and slowly here?

As you continue your walk, now call to mind a fox or a coyote. These animals move through a landscape orienting to the scents of place. Bring attention to your nose and open to the smells of this terrain. You may need to get close to trees, grasses, plants and rocks to sense what fragrance can be known.

Notice what happens when you orient through smell rather than through the dominant sense of sight. How differently do you perceive this landscape? What is revealed when you slow down and attune more subtlety to olfactory experience?

Continue to walk with the influence of these animals, walking slowly and carefully like a lynx, while noticing the varying scents in the air. Now, without losing touch with these more subtle senses, call to mind an owl with their wide, penetrating eyes.

Begin to open up your visual sense. Play with different apertures while seeing. At times, open the panorama of your vision to take in a broad vista. Notice what is happening in the periphery, to the sides, above and below. Feel how it is to walk with this wide-angled vision. Turn your head like an owl, aware of what is all around you.

At times, narrow your vision and bring a penetrating gaze with your eyes, in the same way a hawk pierces a landscape with its detailed vision. Notice the complexity of a blade of grass or a pine needle. Observe the insects on the ground. Can you see the wispy cobwebs floating in the air?

If you feel inclined, you can attune to the sense of touch in the way a snake does with its belly on the earth. You can do this by lying down and feeling the sensations of touch. You can lie face down and sense that intimacy with the ground. Likewise, you can use your hands to touch elements within the landscape, like rocks, lichen, moss, leaves, and bark and feel the environment through sense contact.

Lastly, imagine you are a deer walking through this landscape. With their huge ears revolving like radar dishes, they are acutely attuned to sounds. As you walk, notice the soundscape around you. Listen to near and distant sounds. How do the sounds inform you of what is happening here?

Continue to walk in this way, calling to mind particular animals, birds and other creatures that inspire you in their ability to be present in an embodied, sensory way. Notice how this feels and how it deepens your ability to be present and connected to the natural world. Take the essence of these animal guides with you each time you walk in the wild.

CHAPTER SIXTEEN

STANDING WITH TREES

Trees are poems that the earth writes upon the sky.

— KAHLIL GIBRAN

There are many ways to be mindful in nature. One of those is standing meditation. And, lucky for us, there are an infinite number of teachers that embody this particular form—and they mostly reside in forests!

Trees are perfect exemplars of standing practice. They can inspire us by how deeply rooted and grounded they are, always in intimate connection to the earth. They model an uprightness in their trunks, being always steady but never rigid.

Trees teach us about flexibility, being pliable as they are blown around by wind and storms. They embody a sense of openness as they reach for light and receive the sun's rays.

And they exemplify stillness as they often stand motionless on a calm day.

For this meditation, go outdoors to find a tree that embodies the qualities mentioned above. Before you begin, you may ask permission of the tree to approach and stand with it. You may also bring an offering to the tree, which could be as simple as some water.

Stand in front of the tree, either facing it or leaning against it, or in a position you can sense its presence. Take a moment to gaze at its form, noticing its roots going into the earth, its trunk steady and solid, its branches reaching up to the sky, its leaves opening to sunlight.

Stand with your feet hip-width apart in a stance that feels comfortable and grounded. Make sure your knees are not locked but slightly bent. Have your hands by your side. Then turn your attention inward, and close your eyes or lower your gaze.

Bring awareness to the soles of your feet touching the ground. If comfortable, try this practice with bare feet to connect more intimately with the earth. Sense the contact of the soles of your feet under you. What does the ground feel like?

Imagine your feet are spreading like roots deep into the ground. As you breathe, imagine you are breathing up through the soles of your feet and exhaling back down into the earth through your feet.

Feel your legs like the base of the tree, grounded and supportive of your upper body. Sense your torso lifting like the trunk of a tree skywards. Notice how your spine can be upright but also soft, flexible and responsive to breeze and movement.

Let your arms hang like limbs by your sides. Feel the crown of your head like the canopy of trees oriented skyward. Sense your body like a tree, located between heaven and earth, rooted to the ground yet lifting to the sky. Allow your body to be fluid, letting the body move and sway.

Once you have scanned your entire body, then stand with a general awareness of your body, standing like a tree on the earth. Notice all the physical sensations of this standing posture.

Also be present to the environment around you and how that is impacting your experience. Feel the movement of the breeze, the way a tree senses the wind in its leaves. Notice the presence of sunlight on your body, the way the sun warms the bark of a ponderosa pine. Notice the sounds of the forest and of life around you.

Include awareness of breath as you stand. You may notice how the breath feels different in this posture. Your breathing mirrors the way trees pour out oxygen and take in carbon dioxide. Can you sense how you are literally breathing with trees as you take in oxygen released from their leaves?

At some point you may open your eyes. Take in this tree-being that you have been standing with and who has so much to teach you. Let your eyes gaze at its form, color, shape, texture. Look in detail at the contours of the bark, of the green canopy overhead and its branches stretching up to the light.

You may also wish to move towards it, to touch it, to smell its particular fragrance, or to simply lean against it and feel its steady support and strength.

At the end of the meditation you may offer some gratitude to this tree-being. You may feel this in your heart or offer something in words or in touch.

As you return to your daily activities, know that you can draw on this quality of steady strength, this grounded quality, any time you find yourself standing in your day.

CHAPTER SEVENTEEN
LYING ON THE EARTH

Find your place on the planet. Dig in, and take responsibility from there.

— GARY SNYDER

Awake in the Wild practices can be done anywhere and in all postures. One of my favorite positions for connecting with the earth is through lying down on the ground. Generally we don't associate meditation with being prone on the floor. However, undertaken in the right way, it can be a beautiful form for cultivating qualities of relaxation and providing unique perspectives of nature.

To begin, find a place where you feel comfortable and safe lying down, where you can feel unselfconscious and at ease having your eyes closed. Doing so in a park on a summer's day or on the beach will pass for typical behavior and you should be left alone. But lying down in the privacy of your garden may help you feel more safe.

Once you have found a place, you may want to put a

blanket, towel or yoga mat on the floor, or you can lie directly on the sand, grass or a warm rock. Try supporting your head with a rolled up jacket or cushion. And make sure you are warm enough. You may prefer shade over direct sunlight.

Take some moments to get comfortable in this posture. When comfortable, close your eyes and turn your gaze inwards. Feel the ways your body is touching the earth. Sense your heels, calves, thighs, buttocks, lower back, shoulders, arms, hands and back of your head connected to the earth. Notice where you feel this contact most clearly.

Let your body relax as much as possible. Feel the weight of your body as you rest on and are supported by the earth. Let the weight of your bones be heavy and sink into the ground. Similarly, imagine your flesh and muscles softening and dissolving into the ground. Allow the whole of your body to keep softening. Notice what it is like to feel the entire body relaxing into connection with the earth.

As you breathe, feel the lungs expand with each inhale, pushing your upper back more firmly into the ground. You may feel your back body quite tangibly in this posture. With each exhale soften more into the earth beneath you. If your attention wanders into thinking, notice that shift and return attention to sensing your body.

Continuing to invite ease and relaxation and a sense of melting into the earth. There is nothing to do but lie here, relaxed and alert. At times your attention may be drawn to sounds drifting by or to the breeze on your skin or to fragrance from nature around you. Be present with an attitude of open receptivity to whatever arises in the sensory field.

As you lie there, keep giving your body permission to

rest, to let go, to feel the support of the earth. Practice in this way as long as feels comfortable or interesting.

Towards the end of the meditation, slowly open the eyes and take in the vantage point of the world from the ground —an ant's eye view. What do you see as you look up at the sky, at the clouds, into the canopy of leaves, or at the limbs of trees? How does the world appear from this perspective? Lie here with a soft gaze as you receive the colors, light, forms and movement of the natural world around you.

When you are ready, slowly shift from lying down to sitting or standing. Notice how you feel having laid down on the ground, supported intimately by the earth. What qualities have arisen in this time? Try to take any sense of ease or relaxation with you as you move into the rest of your day.

PART FOUR
NURTURING SENSORY PRACTICES

CHAPTER EIGHTEEN
SENSING THE WORLD THROUGH TOUCH

Touch has a memory.

— JOHN KEATS

Despite having five senses, our miraculous gift of sight is the predominant sense experience and tends to dominate, and even over shadow the other, more subtle senses. In this practice, we will focus on exploring the natural world through the delicate and refined sense of physical touch.

As children, one of the earliest and primary ways we discovered the world was through touch. Infants move through their environment handling, grabbing, feeling, rubbing whatever is at hand. They have a rich intimacy with physical experience.

As we grow older, however, we tend to have less visceral contact with nature and often view it from afar, either through our eyes, or further still via thoughts and ideas. Since moving indoors as a species, we have gotten even further from our once physical, sensory relationship with earth.

To reawaken this sense of touch and to discover the world through fingers, hands and skin is to reawaken a child-like curiosity. Such intimacy can kindle in us a sense of wonder, and surprise and deepen a love for nature.

Begin this practice by going out to a place in nature that is rich with a variety of sensory, tactile experiences. An ideal place may be your garden, but could equally be in a forest, on a beach by a tide pool, or in a city park. One of my favorite ways to explore this practice is with succulent plants.

You can approach this practice in two ways. The first is to do it with a partner. Ask your partner to be the guide and they will take you to different parts of the landscape to explore. You will have your eyes closed and can open to the element of surprise.

The second option is to do the practice solo. You will move through the landscape, stopping when you wish to explore something, and then closing your eyes to enrich that tactile experience.

When you find yourself in front of a flower, plant or tree, begin to sense this unique flora with your hands. Let your fingers and hands move slowly, exploring every shape, crevice, texture and surface of the plant. Notice how it feels to the touch. What does the surface feel like on your skin? Sense its temperature, whether it is cool or warm. Feel whether it is soft or rough, with veins or smooth.

Notice where your curiosity takes you. Let your fingers be drawn along the stems and branches connecting to other parts of the flower or plant. Take a moment to smell this particular expression of nature. How does it feel against the sensitive skin on your cheek?

It's natural for your mind to try to visualize or cognize what it is you are touching, to attempt to classify it or name it. That's perfectly normal, but keep bringing your attention to the immediate sensory contact in your fingers. Know that it takes much longer to explore a plant or flower with your hands than it does with your eyes. So give yourself the luxury of time to fully explore this experience.

Once you feel like you have explored all of a particular plant, then go to another part of the landscape or ask your partner to take you to another mysterious part of nature, perhaps a tree, a shrub, a rock or even some water. Resume this same orientation bringing a quality of "beginner's mind" that is open to the unique sensations that can be felt here.

Let yourself be surprised. Sometimes you may notice a smile or a warm connection for what you are in intimate contact with. Be aware that not only are you knowing this plant, tree or flower, but your presence is also being felt by it as you touch it. You are entering into a relationship of knowing and being known.

Continue this practice for as long as it holds your attention. And if you are doing this exercise with a partner, switch roles. It can be just as fun to be the guide and observe how someone else explores the landscape with their hands and fingers. You can sense the landscape through their own touch and exploration.

CHAPTER NINETEEN
ATTUNING TO FRAGRANCE

Love is like a beautiful flower which I may not touch, but whose fragrance makes the garden a place of delight just the same.

— HELEN KELLER

One of the many gifts of nature is the innumerable scents that can be discovered. Fragrance is a rich, fleeting and precious thing in nature, unique to each flower, tree and forest. It is perhaps the most evocative sense, one rich with memory and meaning.

Our olfactory sense is also perhaps the most depleted and neglected. We live mostly indoors, and aside from our culinary endeavors, there is a limited variety of odor. It is only when we step outside and breathe in fresh air and walk in nature that we realize how diverse and rich the sense of smell can be.

We only have to look at our canine and feline friends, as well as their wilder counterparts—fox, coyote, bear and cougar—to realize there is a whole universe of smell that mostly eludes us. It is another portal into nature's diverse universe that we can explore when we bring a mindful attention outdoors.

You can attune to this sense in meditation by catching wisps of fragrance as you inhale. You can notice smells that drift on the breeze from blossoms, ocean or forest. Meandering while attuning to smell is also a rich and dynamic way to explore this sense faculty.

So find a place where there is a rich variety of smells in a landscape. It may be amidst a garden or a park which has a diversity of plants and trees. It could be along a shoreline or in the woods. Or it could simply be around the streets and gardens in your neighborhood.

Begin by standing or sitting still. Sense your body and breath. Establish mindfulness of breath and attune to physical sensations. Take a few minutes to ground attention in your bodily experience so you feel more present. Then open up your senses to whatever is present here and now. Pay attention to sights, sounds and temperature around you.

Then begin to meander in this particular landscape. Let yourself be drawn to whatever piques your curiosity, to whatever may have a fragrance. Then bring your nose close to this part of nature—leaf, flower, twig, stone, blossom, seaweed etc.

Take some moments to breathe through your nose so the exhale slightly warms this particular leaf or flower. This can help release more fragrance. What are the smells you notice there? Stay close and present to this for at least 30-60 seconds.

Can you notice the variety of smells? Similar to refining your palate as you taste wine or coffee, what are the notes, the range, the variety of fragrance in this particular thing? Perhaps there is an earthiness in the soil. Or a sweet but pungent aroma in the blossom. Maybe in a rotting twig there is a bitter scent but also other qualities.

Our sense of smell is richly evocative, so notice how you may be whisked away to childhood memories of blossoms in your grandparents garden or of playing in the forest or in tide pools when you were young. Notice how those snapshots of time make you feel then come back to this particular scent in the present time.

Once you feel you have fully explored a particular smell, then meander onwards until the next part of the landscape draws you. Let yourself be allured again to noticing the scent of a particular life form.

You may also pick things up from the ground to smell. Or you may rub your fingers on the leaves of bay trees, or sagebrush or any other aromatic plant. Close your eyes and inhale this scent on your fingers. Drink this fragrance in.

At times attune to the aspects of nature you may not expect to have any smell. Does water have a fragrance? What is the aroma of moss or stone? Compare the different smells of tree bark. Does bleached bone give off any scent?

Notice how it touches you as you are smelling parts of nature. What do particular aromas evoke in you? Sometimes they can elicit joy, or curiosity, disgust or desire. Observe how fragrance can stimulate strong reactions and emotions.

Continue your meandering meditation in this way. Keep feeling the invitation to get close, to lean in to smell particular leaves, flowers, bark, sand, stones and anything else that may trigger curiosity. Let yourself have fun with this exploration.

As you end the practice, notice how this made you feel and how perhaps you have a more intimate knowledge or connection with this landscape. Take this attunement to fragrance as you go back into your life and see what can be discovered there through the sense of smell.

CHAPTER TWENTY

EXPLORING THE WORLD THROUGH TASTE

Taste every fruit of every tree in the garden at least once. It is an insult to creation not to experience it fully.

— STEPHEN FRY

We live on an amazing planet that has an extraordinary abundance of wildlife and an incredible array of flora. There is so much in the plant kingdom that offers a feast for our senses. One of those sense avenues is through taste.

Like so many of our sense perceptions, the sense of taste is now mostly confined to eating indoors, to what comes from our refrigerator, pantry or kitchen. It is a rare thing to experience the variety of tastes of nature—like fruits, berries, leaves and other edible plants—when we are outdoors.

In this meditation, you are invited to go outdoors to a garden or a place where you know there are edibles. If there is nowhere in your vicinity to eat something plucked from the ground or a tree, then take something on your walk like a piece of fruit or vegetable to taste as if you had freshly picked it from a tree or from the ground.

Begin this practice by closing your eyes and sensing your body as you sit or stand on this plot of earth. Sense how the body feels here. Feel your breath and notice the quality of air and any fragrance. Then broaden awareness after a few minutes to include the soundscape. Lastly, open your eyes and take in all the color, light and form from this vantage point.

Now begin your meandering walk and orient to what in this landscape may be edible. If you are in your own garden, then let yourself be drawn to where edible plants grow. And if you are walking in the wild, notice any edible fruits or plants (be sure you know what you pluck is indeed edible!).

If you walk in the wild, perhaps in summer, stroll where berries, like blackberries, blueberries, wild strawberries or other fruit grow. Or meander where herbs grow amidst the grasses, like fennel or sage, or where trees offer edible leaves, like bay. Sometimes you may find edible ground cover plants like clover or sorrel.

Once you have found something edible (or if you have brought something with you to taste), take a moment to just look at it. Bring the quality of beginner's mind, as if you were seeing this leaf, fruit or plant for the first time. Notice all its colors, shape and textures.

Notice its aroma. Try rubbing it with your fingers and breathing on it to release fragrance. If you pluck something from a tree, bush or from the ground, first ask permission to take it from its mother plant or tree.

Then close your eyes and place the fruit, berry, leaf or

vegetable in your mouth. Prior to chewing, first sense the texture. How does it feel in the mouth? Is it sweet or bitter, rich in flavor or tasteless? Often it's only by chewing that flavor releases.

Start to chew slowly and mindfully, keeping your eyes closed. Harness your attention and notice the tastes, flavors and smells as you chew. Likewise, as you swallow, continue to notice the flavors and how they change as you eat. Do you discover a surprising taste, sweetness or bitterness?

Continue to taste from the same plant and try to maintain that freshness of attention. We can quickly habituate to sense experience, so the longer we eat or the more we consume of a particular thing, the easier it is to lose the vitality of that first bite.

Once you feel like you have explored this particular fruit, vegetable or plant, then meander again and find another treasure from the trove of nature. Repeat the tasting process just described for as long as feels engaging.

As you finish this meditation, remember to offer gratitude to this abundant earth and to the particular species of plants and trees that you partook from. When you take your next meal, or your next bite of fruit or salad or vegetable, bring the same quality of curiosity to this experience, knowing this too comes from the earth and was once a wild thing growing in the soil.

CHAPTER TWENTY-ONE

LISTENING TO NATURE

The earth has music for those who listen.

— SHAKESPEARE

Perhaps the most quintessential nature practice is listening meditation. When we open attention to the symphony of sounds outdoors, we invite a quality of openness within us. We can't make sounds happen. However, we can relax, open awareness, and simply receive the beautiful sounds that float by.

Listening teaches us a key ingredient in Nature Meditation practice, which is receptivity. We simply put ourselves outside and open up to the myriad sounds nature provides. Listening happens by itself, we simply have to be present for the performance!

Listening practice teaches us to let go of preference, and instead welcome all sounds, even the ones we don't like. We can emulate the way trees openly receive the wind blowing through their limbs, even in the biggest storms. Through doing this we learn the essential skill of being at ease with whatever sounds or other phenomena flow in our direction. This is a great training for life!

Sounds also open our heart to delight. So much joy can be felt listening to the sounds of a trickling stream, to waves on the shore, to the lilting song of birds or the serene rhythm of cicadas at night. What nature sounds are evocative for you?

In this practice, take yourself to a place outdoors where you can easily hear a lively soundscape. Perhaps by the ocean, near a stream, where songbirds abound, or where you can listen to the pitter patter of rain or wind rustling the canopy of leaves. It could even be in the comfort of your own garden.

First, find a comfortable spot to sit. Establish your meditation posture—grounded, upright and relaxed. Close your eyes and sense your body resting on the ground and sense your breath as you begin to cultivate mindful attention here and now.

Then open up your attention to the particular soundscape that is present. Notice all the variety of sounds here. Be present to the general symphony of sounds as if listening to a piece of music. Attune also to discrete sounds that pull your attention within that symphony. Listen to nearby sounds as well as expanding attention to the furthest ones.

It's natural at times to think about what's making the sound, or trying to visualize its source. Often the process of labeling is immediate, especially if you know the songs of particular birds. If that happens, notice the label or image and then let that thought or label go and return to listening directly to the sound itself.

Through hearing meditation you can be mindful of how listening happens all by itself. You only have to relax and be present and sounds are known effortlessly. A bird sings and their song is spontaneously heard. A wave crashes and is felt quite naturally. A dog barks and no effort is required to observe it.

Of course, you will notice other phenomena. You might observe sensations, breathing, light, fragrance, thoughts or movement in your environment. Each time this happens, acknowledge these things and then return to the simple act of listening.

You may also notice unpleasant sounds and how easily we can react to unwanted noise. Observe what happens when you hear the mechanical sounds of planes, cars, sirens, or sounds of music, people or trucks. Can you be like the sky, welcoming all weather, allowing all sounds to be, letting them blow through like the breeze?

From time to time observe the impact sounds have on you. As you listen to the cry of a raven, to the sounds of children playing, to traffic, to the wind howling, what feelings are evoked in that moment? Sounds can be profoundly evocative and remind us how our inner landscape of heart and mind is intimately in relationship to what's happening around us.

Continue to practice in this way for twenty to thirty minutes or as long as it feels engaging. You can solely focus on sounds or you can open up awareness and notice how all experience arises and passes like sounds, coming and going in awareness.

When you draw the meditation to a close, notice how

attuning to sounds can widen the field of perception. Know that you can attune in this way wherever you are and no matter what you are doing. Listening to sounds, whatever they are, is an excellent way to become mindful in the present moment.

CHAPTER TWENTY-TWO

FOCUSING ON THE SOUNDS OF WATER

And gentle winds and waters near, make music to the lonely ear.

— LORD BYRON

The rhythmic sounds of nature can be so stimulating and evocative. Recall times when you've been enchanted by nature's sounds—listening to waves pounding a shoreline, delighting hearing a trickling stream, feeling mesmerized by hailstone on the roof, or loving rain dancing in a canopy of leaves. It could be a time calmed by the pulsing beat of cicadas or the sweetness of a dawn chorus.

These are ways mindful listening happens quite naturally outdoors. However, we can use these same sounds as the focus for meditation. Through listening in this way we can learn how to develop concentration and steadiness but in a very relaxed, open way.

For this practice, go outdoors to a place where you will be able to hear a steady hum of water sounds, like by a cascading stream, a waterfall, by waves lapping the shore-line, or listening to rain or hail hitting a canopy of leaves or landing on a rooftop. And if there is no water near to where you are, you can apply these same instructions to listening to wind.

Find a comfortable place to sit. Close your eyes and take a moment to sense your body sitting on the earth. Notice what the body senses here. Attune also to your breath and take heed of the quality of the air.

Invite as much as you can a quality of ease and relax-ation in your mind and body. Then simply open up atten-tion to the sounds around you. Listen to the symphony of sounds that may be coming to you from all directions. Be aware of the variety of sounds and the silence between them.

Then direct awareness to the sounds of water within the soundscape. Notice the rhythm of waves, the constant trickle of the stream, the drumming of rain. Hold your attention steady there. Let those sounds absorb into you. Let them permeate awareness.

What can you notice about these sounds? What charac-teristics strike a curiosity? Notice how the soundscape is constantly changing, fluid, dynamic. Attune to the loud and subtle sounds, the near and far sounds. Listen as if this was the first time you had heard such things.

When your attention wanders from sounds to thoughts or other phenomena, simply acknowledge this movement, then refocus on the particular sounds you were attending to. You will have to do this many, many times. Know that is part of meditation training, to continually return to the sensory present over and over again.

Notice how listening to sounds can dissolve the notion

of "inside" and "outside." There is simply vibration being known. See how sounds arise and are known quite spontaneously. Try to let go of thinking about and visualizing the source of the sound and let its raw vibration be felt.

Continue to meditate like this, giving your full observation to the watery soundscape. Notice how this feels in your experience as you allow your attention to become solely focused on sounds. How does it feel in your body and mind to absorb awareness in this way?

As you bring this practice to a close, reopen awareness to include other experiences like breath, sensations, smell and lastly sight. Be curious how this style of meditation influences your perception and experience as you move through your day.

CHAPTER TWENTY-THREE

LISTENING TO SILENCE

Listen to silence. It has so much to say.

— RUMI

One of the joys of meditating outdoors is to be able to attune to the beauty of silence. Nature, however, is rarely quiet. There is often a cacophony of sounds from birds, insects, wind and storms. Yet even within that soundscape there is a silence that pervades the natural world which is quite distinct from the flat quiet we may experience indoors.

Some landscapes have a quietude that is almost deafening. The silence in the desert feels distinctly ancient. Perhaps it is because that sandy ground was once an ocean floor. While leading retreats in the red rock canyons of Navajo country, the silence touched there felt timeless, as old as the hundreds-of-million-year-old cliffs.

So too meditating high in the mountains, far from the maddening cry of the city, the silence can feel like a portal to mystery. This quiet presence can open one to sacred dimensions of experience. Mystics for centuries have known this, whether they be Taoist hermits in ancient China, Buddhist yogis of Tibet, or Hindu sages in the Himalayas.

And yet, we can also taste this quality of silence in an old redwood grove, in the stillness of the night or beside a lake at dawn. Perhaps you have the good fortune of living in the countryside where quietude is always available.

In this practice we will explore opening to the sacred quality of silence wherever we are. If you know of a place to meditate that is quiet, then take your practice there for this session.

Begin by finding a comfortable posture where you can sit with ease. Take some moments to orient to this particular place, taking in the sights, sounds, smells, colors and movement. What is the particular quality of this place?

Then close your eyes and orient the body towards the stillness around you and how that can evoke stillness within you. Now open awareness to the silence that is present. Pay attention to its particular qualities. Observe what happens when you attune to the silence. Does it evoke a quality of depth, quietude, stillness or spaciousness?

Of course there will be sounds that emerge in the environment. You cannot help but notice those. However, pay more attention to the way sounds emerge from and return to silence. Also observe the space between sounds and how that is another doorway to silence.

Sometimes you may become aware of the "nada" sound. The nada sound is the sound of silence that you may hear in your ear as a high-pitched tone. It is different than tinnitus. We can become aware of this when the silence is deep and pervasive and when we are present rather than lost in thoughts. If you notice that high-pitched sound, simply attune to it as it ebbs and flows. This too can be a beautiful way to enter more deeply into silence.

As you sit, many sense experiences may pull your attention. Acknowledge these when they occur and keep reorienting awareness to the silence, to the backdrop of the soundscape.

Keep attuning in this way to silence, letting its stillness and mystery touch you. After some time, perhaps twenty minutes or so, open up the field of attention to include other sounds and other experience. Notice how listening to silence impacts you.

As you transition from this practice and move into your day, try to attune to the presence of silence and notice how it influences you as you become aware of it. It can become a beautiful doorway to a meditative presence wherever silence is available.

CHAPTER TWENTY-FOUR

SEEING MEDITATION WITH SOFT GAZE

Look deep into nature, and then you will understand everything better.

— ALBERT EINSTEIN

Most meditations are typically done with eyes closed. Yet, when we are outdoors, we wish to take in the world with all of our senses, especially sight, given that the earth offers such a visual feast for the eyes. So many dazzling forms, so many shades of green, such variety of wildlife, such beauty in mountains, lakes, deserts, and flowers. There is no end to the magnificent vistas nature provides. This meditation aims to include this important sense experience.

Because sight is such a dominant sense for us, it tends to overshadow the other senses. We often get lost in what we are looking at and lose touch with our body, breath, and sense of smell and even hearing. So it is helpful to learn

how to meditate with eyes open that also includes awareness of our entire sensory landscape.

With eyes open, we often become quite "busy" looking
around, reaching for a particular experience. In doing so,
we can disconnect from a more receptive meditative attention. In this practice we will explore meditating with soft
gaze, soft eyes. This stance allows you to take in a wide
panorama and be open to the entire field of experience.

Ideally, find a place to do this practice where you can sit
with a broad vista in front of you. That may involve sitting
up a hillside or mountain, in a forest clearing, by a
lakeshore or facing the ocean. You can also do this practice
in a park or even from a deck on your house.

Begin by finding a comfortable posture. Close your eyes
and sense your body in connection with the earth. Attune
to the interior sensations in your body. Absorb attention
into the movement of breath for some minutes.

Then open awareness to the environment. Be aware of
any fragrance in the air as you inhale. Attune to the skin
and sense how it connects you to air, breeze, sunlight,
warmth and coolness. Open attention wider to hearing,
listening to the soundscape.

Once grounded in mindfulness of sensing, breathing,
and hearing, then slowly open your eyes and gaze downwards. Let the eyes be still rather than darting around.
Simply receive the light, colors, shapes, and patterns that
are present.

Be aware that seeing is happening. Notice that it
happens all by itself. You don't have to do anything except
be present to the visual field. Meanwhile, keep some awareness in your other senses.

Now raise the gaze to just below the horizon line. Invite

the eyes to soften and relax. Imagine your eyes are like windows, simply receiving the light, form and color that come to them. If possible, sit with a panoramic vision so you are aware of the periphery and what is in front of you.

To support a wide gaze, lift both index fingers and stretch out the arms in front of you so you can see both hands. Then widen the hands apart so you can just see the index fingers to the sides. Then lower the hands and keep that wide open vista. Keep inviting the eyes to relax and soften as you do this.

Imagine you are like a satellite dish or a sponge absorbing the full panorama of experience—sensing, hearing and seeing. Try to relax and simply receive the entire visual field.

It's natural that the eyes at times will narrow and be drawn to a particular object, like a bird, tree, wave or cloud. Notice this tendency and then open up the field of vision so the gaze is panoramic again. If the eyes get tired, it can help to lower the gaze or to close the eyes for a few minutes and then reopen them.

Rest in meditation like this, open, receptive and aware. After twenty to thirty minutes bring the meditation to a close and notice the influence of this style of practice.

Meditating with eyes open can take some time to adjust to if you are used to meditating with eyes closed. And it can take time for the eyes to relax and be comfortable with this wide, soft gaze.

It can be profoundly helpful to learn how to bring mindful awareness to having the eyes open since this is how we mostly live our lives. Notice as you move through your day how, simply by being present to seeing, you can establish mindfulness anywhere.

CHAPTER TWENTY-FIVE
MINGLING THE MIND WITH THE SKY

Enter the quiet immensity of your own presence.

— JOHN O'DONOHUE

Meditators for millennia have sought refuge in mountains and craggy peaks as a support for meditation practice. Being up high in the mountains gives one a broad vista, especially of the vast expanse of sky. In Tibet, in the Himalayan mountains, yogis have meditated for centuries, developing powerful practices that open awareness to the sky.

In this meditation, we will explore how taking in the vastness of sky is a metaphor and mirror for the nature of awareness itself. Awareness, the knowing quality of mind that makes mindfulness possible, is innate to all of us. It is what allows us to be present, and to know experience fully. It is through awareness that we wake up to reality in the deepest sense.

In this practice, find a place that has a broad vista of

sky, like on a cliff, rooftop or in an open meadow. If possible, sit up on a hillside or mountain. You could also lie down on the earth if you have an unlimited view of the sky. Ideally, sit at a time when the sun is neither too bright nor shining directly at you. Dawn or dusk are excellent times as the light is softer. Please use sunglasses to protect the eyes if needed.

Once you have found a suitable place, settle into your posture, sitting or lying with ease and relaxation. Take some minutes with eyes closed to attune to bodily sensations and to the flow of breath. Then widen attention out to be mindful of the soundscape and other ways you know the environment through touch, smell and the quality of presence here.

Then slowly open your eyes. Let your gaze take in the broad expanse of sky. Sense its limitless quality. Attune to how vast the sky is. Let your attention absorb into this spacious immensity. You don't need to look around, simply allow the eyes to have a relaxed, wide, panoramic vision. The stance is one of receiving the entire sky visually.

Notice how it feels to take in this wide vista of space. How does it feel in your body, heart and mind to take in this limitless spaciousness?

After some minutes, sense the quality of awareness itself that is equally vast, spacious and open. Awareness, like the sky, has no limits, no boundary, no obstruction. Observe how it is simply present, clear, illuminating like a light all that appears within it, to everything that is known.

Now imagine mingling your mind with the sky. Feel how awareness is not separate from the expanse of sky but is one and the same with it. Awareness is a non-dual pres-

ence, it is one with the phenomena within its field of experience. Sense the undifferentiated quality of sky and
awareness.

As you attune in this way, sense your own mind, and
awareness itself, like this vast sky—open, clear, spacious,
unobstructed. Even as clouds, birds or other phenomena
appear within it, they are not separate from this spacious
awareness that is always clearly knowing, cognizant of
what is.

Continue to rest into this spacious awareness, not separate from and as vast as the sky. When the mind gets
drawn into thinking or other experience, notice how this
too is known effortlessly in awareness in the same way
birds are recognized flying through the sky. Then shift the
attention back to observing the sky and sense how awareness mingles with and is at one with the sky, not different
from what is being observed.

Continue to rest in this spacious, knowing awareness, a
mind like the sky—open, clear and vast. If the eyes get
tired, lower your gaze as this brings some relaxation to the
eye muscles. Similarly you can close your eyes for some
moments to rest the eyes. Know that the angle of your gaze
affects the intensity of the practice. If the eyes are lowered
it is more restful, and as you look towards the horizon or
directly up into the sky it can be stimulating to the nervous
system.

At the end of this practice, close the eyes and notice
how this orientation in practice impacts your own being.
Transition slowly from this practice as it can take some
minutes to adjust the eyes. Be mindful how this quality of
spaciousness and vastness is your own nature revealing
itself and may continue to be felt during your day.

CHAPTER TWENTY-SIX

GAZING AT THE NIGHT SKY

Remember to look up at the stars and not down at your feet.

— STEPHEN HAWKING

Gazing up at the infinite dark space of a night sky is an ancient and timeless activity. Humans have been looking skywards for millennia. Staring upwards, we look into the great mystery and attempt to make sense of our place in the universe.

What I love about sky gazing at night is that it's available wherever we are. No matter how dense an urban jungle may be, we can always see a few stars illuminate the darkness, or at least a waxing and waning moon. And my heart never fails to flutter as I behold the beauty of space.

Seeing the infinite night sky can open the mind to feel a sense of immensity, taking us out of the confined quarters we often lie in. We can tap into something much greater than ourselves. We feel how tiny we really are in the unfathomable expanse of the universe. It can help us to put things in perspective and to not take ourselves so seriously!

This meditation is best done at night, away from the glare of streetlights, houses, cars and other light pollution. Ideally, you would be doing this in the countryside or at a beach, far away from the bright city lights. And if that is not possible, it can also be done from your own garden or balcony. It's helpful if this can be practiced on a relatively cloudless night.

Begin by finding a seated posture that is comfortable, where you have an easy vista of the sky. Or you can do this practice lying down on the ground, resting your body on the earth while taking in the full view of the sky above.

First close your eyes and take some minutes to sense your body. Attune to the sensations of sitting or lying, feeling your body supported by earth. Then sense your breath as you breathe in the fragrant evening air. Be mindful how meditating outdoors at night changes the soundscape, the fragrance in the air, and bird and animal activity.

Now gently open the eyes and invite a quality of receptivity as you receive the vista above you. Allow the eyes to soften and open your gaze to a wide, panoramic vision. Relax the eyes so you can see what's in your peripheral view as well as what's in front or above you.

First notice the vastness of space—this infinite blackness that has no beginning or end. Sense the space between stars and how the universe is mostly this immensity of space stretching out in all directions.

Then open to the brilliance of stars that make up our galaxy. Take in their luminosity. What draws your attention? Can you see the dense cluster of stars that comprise the Milky Way? Do satellites or planets hanging in the sky allure awareness?

It's natural that your attention may be drawn to familiar constellations like the Big Dipper. If that happens, try letting go of the concept "Big Dipper" and just see the arrangement of stars. There is *no* Big Dipper in the sky, just a social convention we have agreed on to name a grouping of stars. So too for all the constellations we label in the sky.

Keep inviting the attention to open to the broadness of space. Try orienting to the whole night sky. Imagine awareness as vast as this immense sky. Awareness and what it beholds are not separate.

Observe how opening to this vastness of night sky influences your heart. Do emotions arise as you stare into the void? What do you feel as you sense yourself as a tiny speck of sand in this enormous panorama of space. Sometimes when we look in this way we feel awe, wonder or reverence.

Gazing at the night sky can open us to mystery. If that happens, let that quality permeate you. Sometimes there are no words, just silence. At other times you may feel both small and yet indivisibly connected to everything in the universe.

Let yourself abide in this spacious sky gazing for sometime. When you feel the practice has ended, take your time to move slowly out of the formal meditation. You may wish to journal or reflect on how this practice has impacted you.

And remember, this sky is the infinite ceiling in every room of your life. Take moments every day to appreciate its presence.

PART FIVE
DEVELOPING
MEDITATIVE QUALITIES

CHAPTER TWENTY-SEVEN
ENTERING STILLNESS

Earth teach me stillness, as grasses are stilled with light.

— UTE PRAYER

What initially drew me to meditate in nature was the sense of profound stillness I often felt while sitting by a calm pond, or walking in a quiet forest. Even lying under the cherry blossom tree at the foot of my childhood garden there was something transmitted by the still presence of nature that drew forth the same quality within me.

Mary Oliver wrote in a poem, "Stillness...one of the doorways into the temple." She is pointing to how stillness is one of those precious ways we touch a sense of the sacred. We can intimate something timeless or holy in the same way we may feel entering an old cathedral.

Since we are intimately connected with our environment, the stillness we feel in nature helps permeate and evoke the same within ourselves. The outer deeply influences the inner. So if we desire a counterpoint to the frenzied, busy, rushed pace of life, we need seek no further than a still place outdoors. When we bring meditative presence to that, stillness can wash through us.

In this meditation, find a day and a time when the outer conditions of weather, wind and sounds are more still. Go outdoors to a place that evokes a quality of stillness. That may be beside a calm pond or a quiet meadow. It may be deep in a silent grove of trees or a tranquil garden.

Find a comfortable place to sit in an upright but relaxed posture. Close your eyes and attune to the physical sensations of your body resting on the earth. Sense the stillness in the ground, the steady, stable and unmoving tone of the landmass under you. Notice if that quality can be evoked within yourself. Sit like a mountain, quiet and grounded, and notice if stillness can arise within your own body.

Then open awareness to the felt sense of stillness around you. Where and how do you sense this quality? Do you feel it in the still quality of the air? Perhaps you sense it in the silence, or the space between sounds. Do trees around you exude a still presence? Or perhaps the grasses are stilled with light. Sometimes it is just an energetic felt sense of a place that exudes that calm, quiet presence.

As you sense the outer stillness, notice how the stillness touches and influences you. Can you feel that same quality arising within yourself? Allow your body to orient to stillness so your physical form reflects this.

Observe what interferes with stillness. Most commonly the busy, thinking mind that stirs up agitation, emotions, and dramas can take us far away from being still. As you observe that, release the thoughts and your attention to them and keep reorienting awareness to the stillness that can be tangibly felt within and around you.

Be curious what else supports stillness. Relaxing the muscles and tension in the body can be one doorway into stillness, as can taking long, slow exhales. So too allowing the body to be still. Continue to let yourself be porous so you can soak up the quietude and stillness that nature exudes, like the moss that soaks up the rain.

At times notice that awareness itself is a steady, unmoving presence that has stillness as its very nature. It can be like the quiet, steady point amidst the storm of experience. Rest in this awareness as you sense how the still presence of nature and your own mind are not different.

After twenty to thirty minutes, or a suitable length of time, begin to shift slowly and open your eyes. As you get up and walk, continue to orient to the stillness that is available even within movement and activity.

CHAPTER TWENTY-EIGHT

FEELING THE POWER OF NATURE

Everything in Nature contains all the powers of Nature. Everything is made of one hidden stuff.

— RALPH WALDO EMERSON

Nature is an incredible force. Our planet emerged from the seismic force of exploding stars. Her raw power is evident in erupting volcanoes, in hurricanes roaring across seas, in tornadoes ripping up a landscape, in ocean surf crashing onto shoreline, in the torrential rain of a monsoon, and in earthquakes shuddering everything in their wake.

Feeling nature's power can be awe-inspiring and terrifying. It can transfix our attention and also light up our heart. We are drawn to its power and yet our survival instincts caution us to protect ourselves from these untamed elements. We build walls and fortresses against its wrath but long to see lightning in the sky or hear its deafening thunder.

The renowned environmentalist John Muir saw the beauty and sacred in such forces. During heavy storms in the Sierra Nevada mountains, he was known to climb a tall pine and tie himself to the tree's limbs to feel the storm's strength. We may not go to such extremes, but perhaps we can understand the attraction to such raw, wild elements of the natural world.

In this practice you are invited to seek out the wild potency of nature. This may mean being beside a stormy ocean, going outdoors on a wild, windy day, sitting on a porch listening to thunderstorms or pounding rain and hail on rooftops, or gazing at lightning tearing across a night sky.

It is important that you are physically safe while doing this practice, so take necessary cautions that you are not exposing yourself to danger while meditating. You may choose to do this where you are both protected but still able to feel nature's vigorous energy. Wearing the right clothing to keep you warm and dry can help you relax while still feeling nature's wild elements.

To begin your practice, take your seat outside, in a place where you feel the force of nature. If comfortable, close your eyes and sense the quality of this moment. Notice what you feel as you attune to the earth's power. Is there curiosity, excitement, trepidation or fear?

Turn attention to hearing. So often we feel nature's power through the roar of her soundscape. Listen to sounds that are an expression of this potency, whether that be the roar of ocean, the clap of thunder, wind howling or the pounding of rain. Open your attention to receive both the range and force of these sounds.

Throughout this meditation, be aware of the relationship of inner and outer experience. Each time you hear the strength of nature, in the sound of waves, the gust of wind or rumble of thunder, be curious what that evokes in you. What emotions stir in your heart? What is the body's response to feeling such vigor?

If the potency can be better sensed through the visual field, open your eyes to take this scene in. This may include gazing at lightning as it illuminates the night sky, or seeing trees bend and yield against the force of the gale, or watching sheets of torrential rain fall from the heavens. Again, be curious what that evokes within you. What physical sensations arise as you see this display? How do you feel as you behold this spectacle?

Continue sitting in this way for twenty to thirty minutes or for whatever time period holds your attention. You may also wish to walk to feel more of this potent expression of nature, feeling the wind blowing against your face, rain dancing on your skin. Open to the din of sounds erupting above and around you and how their vibration resonates within.

Open to the raw vitality and sense how this wild power animates your own being. This is the force of life that courses through every living form in the universe. Let yourself drink in the energy and the way it can enliven every cell of your being.

CHAPTER TWENTY-NINE
OPENING TO JOY & RAPTURE

The earth laughs in flowers.

— RALPH WALDO EMERSON

One of nature's perennial gifts is how easily it evokes joy in us. There are so many ways we can be transported into rapture when in a natural environment. For each one of us that portal is unique. In this practice, we will explore ways the natural world inspires delight.

For myself, nature uplifts the soul in countless ways. I only need to pay attention when outdoors and the kindling of my heart is lit with sparks of happiness. From the delight of seeing the first crimson rays of sunrise, to hearing the sweetness of morning song, to watching cumulus clouds billowing in the midday sky. It can as easily be evoked by walking barefoot on moist grass, smelling the fragrance of apple blossom, or when gazing at the moon setting. All day the natural world offers the opportunity for delight.

To turn one's attention to joy is necessary medicine for the soul. We live in stressful times, and our minds are often fixated on the negative, on what is wrong with ourselves or the world. What a contrast, then, to shine the light of awareness on all that is uplifting, to what brings a smile to the heart.

In this practice, go outdoors to a place you know brings joy. It may be as close as your own garden where you are surrounded by the pleasure of plants and flowers. It might be a park where you can relish in a rich variety of birdsong. It could be in a quiet grove of trees where silence and stillness gladdens. Or maybe you feel most uplifted beside water, a trickling stream, a cascading river or beside the ocean.

Once you have found your sit-spot, take some moments to arrive. As you take your seat, open up your senses. What is it that calls to your senses? Let your attention be drawn to whatever brightens your heart. Do you find pleasure in sounds, sensations, smells, sights or colors?

Look around and take in this landscape. Is there a quiet joy in being close to your favorite trees, or beholding the colors of wildflowers? Perhaps the movement of leaves or waves touches you. Or the silhouette of trees evokes rapture. Notice what draws your gaze and let yourself enjoy the beauty of your environment. Notice how it feels to drink in the pleasure of this place with your eyes.

Now close your eyes and become aware of the soundscape. Let your attention be lured by sounds that usher in some new song of delight. It may be the sweet sounds of birdsong or the delicate rustling of aspen leaves that moves you. Perhaps it is the gentle trickle of water or the lapping waves that uplifts. Listen to the sound of silence and the quiet between sounds and how that can touch the heart. Stay curious about how listening can brighten the mind.

Continue to open awareness, this time to the sensory experience of your body. Notice any simple joy as you sit in stillness outdoors. There may be a pleasure feeling the earth beneath you. Or you may feel a quiet delight as you feel the cool breeze kissing your skin. The sun warming you may bring a smile to your face.

Similarly, as you breathe you may inhale the subtle fragrance of blossoms and flowers sweetening the air. You may savor the earthy smell of humus after rainfall or the evocative scent of freshly mown grass. If you are by the ocean you may be enjoying the salty fresh quality of sea air.

Notice this dance of the senses and how each sensory contact can evoke joy, rapture and happiness. Keep attuning in this way to whatever sense experience unfolds, turning your attention to the particular ways the natural world around you is a constant source of delight. All that is required is you pay attention and notice.

As you end this practice, notice how inclining the attention to what evokes joy can instantly change your mood and provide nourishment to your heart. Know that you can do this in any moment, even sitting indoors gazing at a leaf of a house plant, or catching the light illuminating a tree in your garden. Joy is available everywhere, please help yourself!

CHAPTER THIRTY

ABIDING WITH TRANQUILITY AND PEACE

Draw alongside the silence of stone, until its calmness can claim you.

— JOHN O'DONOHUE

Tranquility seems to be a diminishing resource today. We tend to live our lives rushing from one thing to the next. Our minds are often restless, perennially unsatisfied. Our bodies are simultaneously over-caffeinated and fatigued. We live with a low-grade anxiety about time scarcity and the relentless pressure of trying to survive. No wonder we crave peace.

Fortunately nature provides infinite ways to access the beautiful quality of tranquility. Lying on the earth can bring a steadiness that grounds agitation. Ancient trees exude their calming presence. The stillness of a pond transmits a serenity that can soothe the soul. Watching the movement of clouds can evoke ease. What in nature brings quietude for you? Even beholding flowers in a vase can communicate restfulness.

In this meditation, go outdoors to a place where you have been known to access calm. This may be immersing yourself in a woodland, lying on a quiet beach, sitting beside a pond or stream, or visiting a favorite park that evokes tranquility. It could even be resting in your own garden.

As you find a place to meditate, find a posture that most easily allows you to feel at rest, either in a comfortable chair, sitting on the ground, or lying on the earth. As you close your eyes, invite your body to relax. Soften your eye muscles, release your jaw, lower your shoulders and let your belly melt.

Close your eyes. Attune to any quality of calm that may be accessible here. If you sense peace around you, observe how that feels in your body. What happens physically as you attend to tranquility. Notice how outer calmness can influence inner experience. Your breath may lengthen, tension may begin to melt, the racing mind may slow down.

Then be mindful which sense door connects you with the tranquility here. Is it through gazing at the surface of the water, or looking at the still trees? Is it from sensing, through feeling the contact with the steady ground under you? Perhaps it is through listening to silence or the sounds of birds or waves. Maybe it's a whole body experience involving all the senses.

Whatever sense door allows you access to calm, turn your attention there fully. Let your eyes drink in the peacefulness of a pastoral landscape. Listen to the serenity that arises from the sound of water. Feel into the quietude of silence. Lean into a particular tree as you connect with its still presence. Allow your body to dissolve if lying on the earth brings ease.

Continue to attune in this way. Stay curious how you feel this tranquility in the outer landscape and how this has a calming influence on your mind and body. As peace grows within you, attune to the quality of tranquility itself, feeling into the stillness and calm it brings. Doing so can allow this soothing quality to flourish.

Be observant with what interferes with calm. Most commonly it is the busy mind with its thoughts, worries and plans, taking you far from the tranquility of the present moment. Each time you catch yourself pulled into the agitation of thought, simply release the thought and reorient to the inviting calm of nature.

As you draw this practice to a close, reflect on the impact that attuning to tranquility in the outer and inner landscape has. Know this quality is available anytime we choose to turn towards it, when we orient to what abides with such peace.

CHAPTER THIRTY-ONE

CULTIVATING FOCUS AND CONCENTRATION

For every moment of concentration there is an equal moment of relaxation.

— DERREN BROWN

There are two distinct ways to cultivate mindfulness meditation. One is to focus the mind to a narrow point, to concentrate on one particular object like breath. The other is to broaden attention, to be present with an open awareness, present to the whole field of experience.

Much of nature meditation practice, and many of the meditations in this book, utilize the latter, this open receptive quality of attention, sometimes called "open" or "choiceless" awareness. However, there is much value in honing attention to a single point, to develop the art and skill of focus.

In this practice, you are invited to attend single-pointedly to one particular thing. Traditionally, the breath is used as a concentration object. But here, you will use something in nature. It may be something visual like a leaf, a flower, or the bark of a tree. It may be a discrete sound like the crashing of waves or the fall of rain. It may be the movement of air on your skin as you sit outdoors on a breezy day.

Ideally, you choose something that can hold your attention steady for some time. In different meditations you can experiment with using either a visual object, an auditory one, or one that explores the sense of touch.

In this particular meditation, close your eyes and turn attention to your breath. Allow a natural steady focus to arise by absorbing attention into the sensations of breath as you inhale and exhale. Bring a quality of beginner's mind as if this was the first time you had experienced breathing.

The key principle with concentration practice is to both absorb attention into the chosen object and to recognize each time the mind has wandered away. Then simply return focus over and over to the given object, in this case the breath. You may choose to stay attuned to breath for the entire practice.

As a way to explore the range of what you can focus on, once you feel your attention is steady, shift to attune to sensations of touch. Sense a particular place on your body in connection with the earth. Absorb awareness into these sensations.

Cultivating curiosity to experience is what allows us to sustain focus. It engages our attention. Alternatively, you can focus on the sensations of breeze on the face if you are outdoors on a windy day. Stay intimately present to these changing sensations of touch.

After some minutes open the eyes and bring that same

focused attention to a single point. It may be to a leaf, a stone, tree trunk or flower. This will be the focus for the remainder of the meditation so choose something that will easily hold your attention.

Again, let your attention absorb into this experience of the leaf or flower. Turn the gaze to explore it intimately and take in its color, shape, form, texture and light. What else can you know and sense about it? Bring a quality of beginner's mind so you experience it anew, as if for the first time.

Each time your mind gets bored or your attention wanders into thought, or starts to look around or drift into some other experience, acknowledge that and resume your focus on this visual experience. Do this in a way that is patient but persistent.

Know that concentration deepens through relaxation and pleasure. So ensure you are at ease as you do this, not forcing or pushing or straining. And be mindful to include what may be pleasurable within this experience. What color, shape, form or texture can be appreciated as you absorb into it? What can be learned as you study this with all your attention?

Continue to focus in this way. By doing this you can learn to cultivate a calm and steady mind through concentration. And as much as there is a variety of experience and stimulation outdoors, we can still learn to develop a focused mind anywhere in nature.

CHAPTER THIRTY-TWO

OPENING INTO SPACIOUS AWARENESS

Nature is an infinite sphere of which the center is everywhere and the circumference nowhere.

— BLAISE PASCAL

As pointed out in the previous chapter, there are two principal orientations to practice. The majority of meditation techniques involve focusing the attention to a single experience, like to breath, a mantra or a sensation. In contrast, open awareness, which is an essential mindfulness practice, draws on a natural, spacious quality of mind, in which one meditates with a 360-degree perspective, open to all experience.

The beauty of this style of practice is it is perfectly suited to being outdoors. When we are in nature, our attention is organically drawn to a wide variety of stimuli. We can simultaneously be aware of light coming through clouds, breeze rustling leaves, sounds of birds calling from treetops, as well as the smell of the forest we are walking through and the touch of the earth underfoot.

In this practice, find a place in nature where you know you will be exposed to a broad range of experience. Then take your seat, close your eyes and settle awareness into the felt sense of sitting. Notice the multitude of sensations from just sitting on the earth.

To invite this attitude of open awareness, turn attention to hearing and open to the kaleidoscope of sounds coming above and below you, from behind and in front of you, and all around. Listen to the symphony of sounds. Sounds ceaselessly appear and disappear in this open field of awareness. Sounds arise and are effortlessly known with attention.

Imagine you are like a satellite dish, receiving signals from all directions. Awareness is like this, receptive and open. No need to reach out to the sounds or make them happen. Simply relax and observe.

Let go of thinking about the sounds or visualizing their source and instead attune to the raw sound, the vibration itself. Continue to rest in this natural knowing awareness of hearing, present to sounds appearing like bubbles rising in a spring.

Expand the field of awareness to include how other phenomena arise and pass in awareness. Be present to myriad physical sensations as the body touches the earth, how skin contacts the air. Notice any inner sensations of tingling, vibration, or pressure and how they too are felt pulsing in awareness.

As you breathe, sense the sensations of cool air as you inhale. Observe how smells, fragrance and scents of the earth are similarly known as they appear.

As you rest in open awareness, notice how changes in temperature, warmth and coolness are naturally felt. So too movements of air, breeze and wind are simultaneously known. Changes in light, as the sun moves in and out behind clouds, are sensed effortlessly.

As you abide in open awareness, be present to the ever-changing display of nature through the senses of hearing, sensing, smelling and touch. You can also include the inner landscape. Notice when strong emotions and moods arise, like weather patterns, like storms, and notice how they are felt in the body. Thoughts, images and ideas may also drift through the mind and can be equally known in the same way sounds are felt.

Lastly, sit with a broad awareness as vast as the sky, present to the entire field of experience that can be known around you. Note how awareness and that which is known are not separate. Continue to rest in this natural, spacious quality of mind for as long as feels comfortable. Then open the eyes and include the sense of sight. Notice how awareness has the ability to notice an entire panorama of experience receiving them all through the eyes, and being known spontaneously and effortlessly.

As you end this practice, notice the impact of meditating in this way. As you continue your day, know that you can bring this same quality of spacious awareness into whatever it is you do.

CHAPTER THIRTY-THREE
RESTING IN NON-CONCEPTUAL AWARENESS

We depend on nature not only for our physical survival, we also need nature to show us the way home, the way out of the prison of our own minds.

— ECKHART TOLLE

As human beings, we live in a world mediated through our concepts and ideas. We are masterful at cognition, at understanding experience through our minds. The natural sciences profoundly expand our knowledge of flora and fauna on earth, refining our comprehension about ecosystems, geology and countless species.

However, what can become occluded with such knowledge is a more immediate, intimate, sensory experience of life. We may listen to morning birdsong more to identify the birds than to hear exquisite sounds. We walk through a field of wildflowers, keen to classify them and remember their Latin names. We behold an oak tree, not looking beyond the name we give it. We taste a wild mushroom and are lost contemplating mycelium networks.

To be in nature and only know it through concepts is to limit our experience. Such ideas are helpful to a point. However, it is essential we springboard from these perceptions and enter a more intimate relationship with the earth if we are to know it fully and receive its beauty, mystery and wonders. Non-conceptual orientation can help with that.

You can do this meditation while sitting, but I suggest for this practice you meander through a landscape, neighborhood, garden or park. Doing so in a place where you know the species of plants, trees, birds or animals is helpful.

To begin, take a few minutes to cultivate a mindful attention. Either in a seated posture or standing, close your eyes and sense the feet firmly on the ground. Release concepts of your body and feel the immediacy of physical sensations.

Observe how the body registers the environment through sensing temperature, air, breeze, fragrance, movement. Be aware of breathing without any image or label of breath. How do you feel it viscerally?

Now open your eyes and begin to move around the landscape. Visually take in this place, paying attention to flora. Stand in front of a plant you know. The name of this species may immediately arise. Acknowledge this and then study this plant's particularity beyond the label given to it.

When cultivating a non-conceptual awareness, try to shed concepts, stories and memories and instead bring other senses into play. Notice the colors and varieties of forms of this plant. Observe the layers and shades of green.

Study its various textures. Touch a leaf and feel its temperature, the smoothness or roughness of its surface. Smell any aroma that it exudes. Can you feel its presence, energy or life force?

After a time, walk to a nearby tree you recognize. Bring the same fresh, receptive quality of attention. Notice the naming of this species. Acknowledge this process, then shift to experiencing "tree" through the senses.

Begin by visually studying the tree. Notice its root structure. Gaze into the canopy and the limbs that reach skyward and how they bend and twist to do so. Observe the variety of colors and shades of green, brown and gray. Bring curiosity to the texture of the trunk. Is it gnarled or smooth, contoured or ruffled?

Engage the sense of touch and begin to explore the tree's surface. Notice how roots, trunk and branches may have their distinct tactile quality. Be mindful of any smell of the bark and leaves. What else can you sense about this particular tree?

Once you feel complete with each flora you study, move onto the next part of the landscape. Bring this same non-conceptual mode of attention to a rock, a stone, an animal or insect.

Similarly, as you listen to the sounds of birds, observe the mind's swift labeling of the species. Release the concept and simply listen to the call of the bird or its song. You can do the same with any scent or fragrance you recognize and label.

Continue to track how rapidly the mind labels phenomena and then thinks about it. Such reflection has its uses. However try to release such contemplation and instead bring a full sensory engagement with whatever it is you are with.

Let yourself fully take in each new experience fully, free from your ideas, memories and stories about it. See how differently you may apprehend the world and how doing so can enrich and deepen your connection in nature.

As you close this practice, know that you can also bring this non-conceptual perspective to observing people, buildings, cars—anything. Be curious what this opens up as you take in experience in a non-conceptual way.

PART SIX
MEETING ADVERSITY

CHAPTER THIRTY-FOUR

STEADYING LIKE A MOUNTAIN (EQUANIMITY)

There is a huge amount of freedom that comes to you when you take nothing personally.

— DON MIGUEL RUIZ

It is remarkable how resilient the earth is in the face of seismic challenges. This planet has gone through metamorphoses through explosive combustion, molten heat, volcanic eruptions, ice ages, tectonic plates colliding and more. Yet throughout all of it pervades a stillness and steadiness.

So much life on earth embodies this same strong presence. The quiet majesty of ancient trees, ancient canyon walls and the resolute steadfastness of mountains to name a few. They are quiet teachers of equanimity, with the ability to be spacious and steady amidst life's vicissitudes.

Not long ago I spent some weeks trekking around Mt. Manaslu in Nepal, standing more than eight thousand meters tall. What impressed me most was that majestic peak's profound silent presence. It annually endures bitter winter storms, torrential monsoons, avalanches, rock slides, erosion and yet stands quiet and immovable.

Spending time near the magnificent stature of mountains, something of their presence transmits itself to us. We may feel the same steadiness standing with a towering oak tree, by lying on an ancient river bed or gazing at vast stone cliffs.

In this meditation you will learn to draw on nature to develop the beautiful quality of equanimity, which provides the capacity to meet experience with spaciousness and ease. This training to meet the changing elements outdoors helps us meet inevitable challenges we encounter in life.

The intention of this practice is to access steady presence, the way trees meet the storms that blow through the forest and how mountains receive any weather. Ideally, try this practice on a windy day or where there is some wild weather, perhaps sitting amidst showers or hail or snow. However, make sure you do this in a safe way.

Begin by going outdoors to a place you can sit in a natural landscape where you feel the strong presence of the natural world, whether that be from trees, mountains, ocean, rocks or similar forces of nature.

As you take your meditation seat, sense your rooted connection to the ground. Feel your sit bones entwined with the solid earth under you. Sense how the earth has been this stable presence for millions of years. Notice if you can feel that same steady presence with yourself.

In the same way feel the reliable presence of your breath, dependable and rhythmic. Sense how the stillness between breaths mirrors the stillness of earth. Know that you can draw on this calm pause in any weather, in any circumstance.

As you attune to the changing elements around you, notice there is almost always a variety of both pleasant and unpleasant, wanted and unwanted experience. This may come in the form of heat or cold, or oscillate between windy and calm or discomfort and ease.

Just as the spacious sky accommodates all weather that passes through it, sense how your own awareness has the same capacity to receive all experience. It remains open and receptive to everything, including the changing conditions and unpleasant or unwanted phenomena without reacting.

If you are out on a windy day, as cold air blows, or strong gusts howl around you, see if you can embody the receptive presence of trees. They remain still, yet fluid, responsive and yielding as they allow the force of winds to blow through their limbs. Sometimes, the stronger the wind around you, the more steady you may feel in meditation, rooted in place, able to simply receive what comes.

You can bring this steadiness to the fluctuation of temperature, where cold breeze chills the skin, and sun bakes it. Or where drizzle or fog dampens your hair and moistens your clothes. Sense how mindfulness helps you simply meet and receive any weather. You may prefer some sensations over others, prefer cozy warmth over chills, but awareness stays at ease in the midst of such changes.

Continue to draw inspiration from natural elements around you that abide with steady presence no matter the circumstances. Know that the basis for equanimity is a radical acceptance—a willingness to simply be with what is, both in meditation and in life. Sense how you can draw on nature's ability to remain with such presence in any situation.

As you leave the meditation, know that you can bring this same quality of steadiness to what life has to bring you wherever you are.

CHAPTER THIRTY-FIVE

ACCEPTING WHAT IS

It is not the sounds that disturb us, it is we who disturb the sounds.

— ACHAAN CHAH

As much as we relish being outside, there are often challenges involved with being in nature. Outdoors we can be exposed to raw elements, raging storms, wild animals, biting insects and other adversities. Hence the reason we like the warm, cozy, protected spaces of our homes. Yet they don't bring us the aliveness and joy the same way being outside does.

How often have we been trying to swat and repel buzzing insects around us only to attract more of them to swarm? Or have been complaining about airplane traffic and created more noise in our head than the sounds! So often our reaction to unpleasant experience outdoors creates more waves than the thing we are not liking.

But when we learn to mindfully welcome *all* experience

in nature, this attitude helps us be at peace no matter what.vTo meditate outdoors means being present with everything, including our reactions to what is happening. This means not just tolerating discomfort but opening to it as a vital part of our meditation journey.

You'll want to engage with this practice on a day when you know the weather, bugs, sounds or other things may be not to your preference. Perhaps you choose a cold or sweltering day, one where conditions are not to your liking —which could be many days of the year!

Begin by finding a comfortable posture as the area affords. Close your eyes and sense your body's connection to the ground. As much as possible, invite the body to relax. Attune to your breath, sensing the releasing quality of the exhale.

Allow attention to breath to be your anchor for the meditation, and whenever your mind drifts into thought or you get reactive to some experience, come back to sensing breath as a way to stay centered during those times.

After some minutes, open attention to the soundscape. As you listen, most likely there will be a variety of sounds both pleasant and unpleasant. Try to open to all sounds even if they are jarring or loud. Be mindful when you can accept what is, it becomes easier to tolerate experience.

Now attune to the changing temperatures. Perhaps you are meditating on a bitingly cold day or on a hot, sunny afternoon. As your body heats or cools, notice the uncomfortable sensations that this brings. When you sense the unpleasantness in the body and accept it, not trying to make it different, notice how that can bring more ease in relationship to it.

Similarly, if you are sitting on a blustery day, be present

to the strong wind and gusts as they blow. Feel the full force of the wind as it blows against your body, face and hair. Notice if you can be present to both the wind and what it evokes in you. Can you embrace the breeze and your reaction to it, particularly if you are resistant or recoiling from it? Draw on the support of nature by imagining yourself like a mountain or ancient tree, simply receiving whatever comes its way.

Lastly, bring awareness to the insects and bugs that may plague you as you sit. Notice the sounds and the way ants tickle the skin or bugs try to bite it and see what that stirs up in you. Take care of yourself as needed, by applying insect repellent prior to meditating or wearing a mosquito head net.

Nevertheless, bugs will still come, so see if you can simply notice their sounds and presence. Can you bring a quality of acceptance that they too are part of nature and have equal right to be here with you in this environment? And if not, notice what else is present.

Continue to practice in this way, open to all the wild and wonderful ways nature can challenge our practice. Keep orienting to the intention of accepting what is happening both outwardly and inwardly. Observe how doing so can strengthen your ability to be present to all conditions.

CHAPTER THIRTY-SIX

CONFRONTING FEAR— MEDITATING AT NIGHT

The darkness will be your womb tonight, giving you a horizon further than the eyes can see…

— DAVID WHYTE

As much as we may love nature, it harbors experiences we are often afraid of and intimidated by. In my early years of wilderness exploration, I was afraid of the dark and camping out alone. My mind conjured terrifying scenarios. Being alone at night in the forest, a rustle in the bushes would trigger fears of hungry bears or prowling cougars.

As I've spent more time in the wilderness on solo backpacking trips, I've come to realize that humans are much more of a threat to wildlife than they are to us, and most creatures are happy to keep their distance. I've come to embrace, instead of fear, both the dark and solitude. The night hours are a time to enjoy the stillness and starry skies.

With mindfulness and kindness, we can learn to work with our fears and trepidations about being outdoors alone or at night. In this practice you are invited to explore your comfort zone and work with whatever feelings arise as you meditate outside during the dark hours.

Begin by reflecting on where would be a safe place for you to explore working with fear. Perhaps sitting outside at night in your garden is your "edge," that place that takes you to the limits of your comfort. Or perhaps meditating outside of your tent at night on a camping trip is a stretch. Maybe going out in the light of the full-moon in a park is a good place to start.

Wherever you choose, pay attention to how you feel. As you head outside into the dark, try to go without light or use a red light so you don't lose night vision. Notice what emotions are present in your heart. Try to name them and sense them physically. If you sense agitation, fear or anxiety, try bringing kindness to yourself as a way to invite ease.

Observe what you sense in your body and whether any tension is present. If possible, try to invite a quality of relaxing. Feel your feet on the earth as a way to ground. Take longer, slower exhales, which can help bring ease to the nervous system. Softening areas in the body that become tense can also ease the nervous system and heart.

As you take your meditation seat on the ground or on a log or rock, look around you and see what can be noticed in the darkness. Perhaps silhouettes of trees or the night sky. If it is more comfortable, keep your eyes open, resting the gaze downwards.

Sense your body resting on and supported by the earth. Feel the supportive quality of that contact. Then open to the night soundscape around you. Be aware of the silence and the sounds that emerge. Notice any pleasurable sounds that may evoke ease and be curious if the silence is comforting.

Throughout this meditation, stay present not just to external stimuli but also how you feel in relation to being outside at night. If fear arises, notice what you are afraid of. In particular, observe if the mind is creating scenarios that unnecessarily conjure anxiety or fear. Shift attention away from thinking and sense your breath. Keep turning your attention to what allows you to feel calm or grounded.

Another practice that can help is to sense the benevolence of the natural world. Nature is generally welcoming of our presence. Can you feel your love and care for the trees around you, for the birds nesting in the canopy, for the creatures sleeping underground? Radiating warmth and care for the life around you is a powerful antidote to fear.

Continue in this way for as short as a few minutes or for longer, perhaps twenty to thirty minutes. Do as much as you can relaxing into the experience. As you continue to do this practice, you may find your ability to tolerate the dark or being outdoors alone increase. You may find your fear changing and lessening. You may even begin to relish the quiet darkness of the night. And if it feels like too much, you can always retreat to the safety of your home or to the comfort of company.

In your life, you may try to work with other things that provoke fear. You may experiment, as in this meditation, to turn gently towards situations, people or experiences that cause fear. Using breath and grounding techniques can help you find centeredness in such situations.

PART SEVEN
CULTIVATING INSIGHT

CHAPTER THIRTY-SEVEN

CONTEMPLATING THE FOUR ELEMENTS

You are water, I'm water, we're all water in different containers.
That's why it's so easy to meet. Someday we'll evaporate together.

— YOKO ONO

When we can walk through a forest or along a beach it is easy to sense how different it is from us in size, shape, color, texture and movement. However, dig a little deeper and we realize we are made of the same stuff as rocks, trees, shells, ocean and clouds. How is that?

Eastern spiritual traditions for millennia have pointed to how the four elements of earth, air, fire and water reveal the inherent connection that unites all life. There is so much more that connects rather than divides us.

We may know how a leaf is formed from earth, water, air and fire (sunlight) but this is equally true of our own body. In this meditation you will attune to the elements within you, which can help bring a greater sense of inter-connection with all life.

Begin this meditation by going outdoors. As you take your seat, look around. Notice the trees, grasses, rocks, clouds and plants. Sense how all life is created by and are expressions of all the elements.

Now close your eyes and sense your body on the earth. Feel the contact with the earth element, the ground under you. Sense how you are part of the earth's surface, seated and aware. The earth under you and the rocks, hills, mountains, trees and creatures are all made of the same earth element.

Reflect how we all come from the earth, we eat and digest the earth element, we excrete the earth element, and eventually we return to the earth at death. We are never for a moment separate from the earth.

You can sense the earth element directly within you as hardness, density, heaviness and solidity. Feel now your bones, your knuckles, skull, teeth, jaw, fingers and ribcage. This hard mass is the earth element. So too are your flesh, organs, skin. Take some moments to feel that. Notice what happens when you sense that the earth element within you is the same element in rocks and mountains, not separate.

After a few minutes, shift attention to noticing the water element. We are made of more than seventy percent water. The water in the rain, clouds and lakes is not different from the blood in our veins. Our tears reflect the saltiness of the ocean. We sense water through moisture, sweat, saliva, and fluidity in our joints and in our intestinal tract.

Sense directly the water element within your body. Feel the blood moving as the heart pumps. Notice the wetness of your eyes and mouth. Feel moisture on your skin and fluidity in your joints. The water element outside in clouds and oceans is the same as the water element inside. Not separate.

Now turn awareness to breath. The air element around you is the same air you inhale. The oxygen in the air is vital to every biological process within you. With each breath you inhale oxygen released from forests and plankton. Each exhale you breathe out is carbon absorbed by plants and grasses. With each breath, sense how the air element outside and the air element within you is the same element. Not separate.

Lastly, sense the warmth in your belly, the heat of your torso and coolness of your skin. That heat in the body is not separate from the fire element of the sun, 93 million miles away. We come into this life as a warm-blooded mammal. We retain that heat by digesting and absorbing energy from plants that have harnessed the light of the sun. And when we die, that fire element quickly leaves us. Sense now the warmth of your body and the heat of sunlight. Know how they are connected to the one same fire element. Not separate.

Lastly, be aware of the flow of elements, how they can be felt simultaneously as this flow of inner experience of hardness, density, fluidity and wetness, warmth and coolness, and the inhale and exhale. Know how these are intimately connected to the elements all around you.

After you end this practice, notice the impact of this reflection. See if it changes your sense of connection and belonging as you realize everything around you is made of the same stuff of life.

CHAPTER THIRTY-EIGHT

UNDERSTANDING TRANSIENCE

What we conceive is ever other than is so.

— BUDDHA

W hat in this world lasts? I gaze at the hills and rocky crags before me that have seemingly remained the same for the two decades I've walked here. Yet, are they really continuous? If I look closer, the solid crags crumble little by little every year. The gulleys made by winter runoff widen gradually over time. And the hillsides are an ever-changing landscape of green in winter, then golden brown after a dry summer. What seems solid and permanent is anything but.

We know intellectually that everything changes. Yet we often relate to life blinded by that truth. We get upset when we lose things, get attached to things that we know will change, and react to life's inevitable losses. I lament every time the verdant grassy hills turn golden even though

I know they will. A conceptual grasp of transience is not enough. We need to grasp it deep in our being.

Nature is a masterful teacher of the truth of change. Nothing stays the same in nature. We can see this in the ephemerality of clouds, the elusiveness of scents, the ebb and flow of waves, changing weather, shifting seasons and now the ever-changing reality of climate change.

Paying attention to transience in the natural world helps us deeply know this in the fabric of our being. It invites us to live more lightly and with more ease with the changing fluctuations of life. We can similarly notice the ephemeral experience within our own mind and body and hold that more wisely.

In this meditation, go outdoors to a place where it is easy to feel changing experience. This could be going out on a windy day, or to a place where there are obvious changes in the soundscape, like by the ocean or a stream.

As you take your seat, close your eyes and turn your attention to hearing. Notice how sounds ceaselessly appear and disappear. No two sounds are the same, no soundscape is unchanging. Listen to how sounds teach you about transience. No sooner does a sound arise than it changes, passes away. Try to notice the endings of sounds as they fade. Let hearing be the anchor for this meditation.

As you open to the changing sounds, also include other phenomena. Bring awareness to how the skin is often registering the moving air, fluctuating temperature, warm sunlight coming and going and the caressing breeze or the wind's ebbs and flows.

Similarly, include awareness of your body's changing landscape. Notice how sensations are forever changing, intensifying, ceasing. No two moments of physical experience are the same. In the same way, feel the perennial waves of breath that are never stationary.

So too with our thoughts, feelings and moods. Be mindful how our inner mental and emotional landscape are always in motion, constantly influencing each other. Even more so, note how thoughts reflect the very temporal nature of experience, forever flickering in and out.

Continue to notice this ever-changing inner and outer landscape, attending to whatever is most predominant in each moment, different from one moment to the next.

Finally, open your eyes and bring mindfulness to seeing. Notice how, even though things appear fixed and solid, there is often change occurring in light, movement, color, texture and shape. Clouds morph, leaves rustle, birds flutter overhead.

Nothing in this world stays the same. The more we attune to that in the natural landscape the more we can know this experientially and not be surprised or taken off guard when things change or dissolve in our life. We realize there is nothing, ultimately, to hold on to.

Continue to practice in this way for twenty to thirty minutes. As you end the practice, notice the influence of orienting to change in this way. As you go back to your other activities, be mindful how change is everywhere and how you may relate to it differently as you become more conscious of this ever-changing reality.

CHAPTER THIRTY-NINE

INTERCONNECTING WITH ALL LIFE

Touch one thing in the universe and everything moves.

— JOHN MUIR

Einstein once wrote that we live in an "optical delusion of consciousness." When we look out at the world, it seems to be made up of discrete objects, things that are entirely separate from each other. Our eyes aren't able to see the innumerable hidden connections that bind us all.

Trees look separate from the air, from the sun, from each other. Yet when we look closer, we see how they live within an intricate web of connection with life around them. Trees are constantly absorbing carbon from the air and exuding oxygen. They are connected underground by miles of mycelium networks, sharing nutrients and information. The sun, so far away yet indispensable to the tree's life.

This is true of every living thing. We all live within vast

ecosystems that are mutually supportive. Yet it is easy to feel cut off from this web within our homes and offices, to feel separate from broader forces around us. This is why going outdoors is essential to understanding our place in the matrix of life. Otherwise, as humans we risk the hubris of thinking that we can act independently without having impact. To do so, of course, is at our own peril, as we are now seeing ecologically.

Begin this practice by going outdoors and sitting in a place where you feel immersed in the elements of nature. As you sit, look around at the natural beauty around you. Notice whether you feel connected or separate from it. Whether it feels kin or "other."

Now close your eyes and sense your body resting on the earth. Reflect how you are always in contact with the ground. You are part of the earth's moving surface. Notice what happens when you sense that connection.

Turn attention to your skin. Observe how this organ reminds you of your connection to the world. Feel how skin is a bridge to the air around you, to its moisture or dryness. Sense how, through skin, you can know the breeze and the atmosphere around you as well as changing temperatures. Sense how your skin registers, at times, the sense of threat, of animals nearby, again attuning you to the environment.

After some minutes, bring awareness to breathing. Sense how each inhale brings you in intimate contact with the air around you. Notice the fragrance that may reflect the flora nearby. Feel the moisture in the air, indicative of the weather systems and seasons you are in.

Be mindful how, with each inhale, you are breathing in oxygen released from trees in the Congo, the Amazon rainforest, from grasses in Canada, from plankton in the Indian Ocean. With each exhale the carbon released by breathing is reabsorbed by plants and shrubs everywhere. Observe how you feel when you sense you are breathing with all breathing life, all photosynthesizing life.

After some minutes open awareness to sounds. Notice how the senses are intimately bridging the inner and outer worlds. Feel how listening connects you to the soundscape created by birds, insects, wind, water and storms. Observe how mindful listening conjoins you with the life nearby.

As you sense the moisture in your body—sweat, tears, blood—be aware that all the waters in your body come from rain, snowmelt, storm clouds, oceans. You are a skin-bound ocean. The fluids that pour through your veins are not separate from the streams and rivers of the earth.

For a moment, reflect on your connection to all the beings, to humans and the more than human world that have been present in this place, all the myriad life forms that have lived or moved through here. In some ways you are connected with them also.

Meditate in this way for twenty to thirty minutes, feeling all the ways your body and senses connect you to the environment. Toward the end of the practice, open your eyes and notice if you feel any more a part of or closer to the life around you. Continue this awareness as you move through your day, observing ways you are connected to life around you.

CHAPTER FORTY

DISSOLVING BOUNDARIES OF SELF

The birds have vanished into the sky. The last remaining clouds have faded away. We sit together the mountain and me, until only the mountain remains.

— LI PO

Earth teach me to forget myself as melted snow forgets its life.

— UTE PRAYER

One of the hidden joys in nature is we come into the presence of wild things who are not lost in stories and drama about themselves. Stepping away from the human, ego-centered world, we enter a natural habitat that is peaceful, free from the fretting and angst about "me" and "my life" that engulfs most of us a lot of the time.

As we immerse more outdoors with mindful awareness, we can momentarily and happily put our personal narratives down and instead literally lose ourselves inside a sensory world. We enter fully into the moment, not lost in machinations about our own dramas, but instead absorb into nature's beauty and serenity.

Even momentarily releasing our self-preoccupation, releasing the sense of "self" in favor of being fully attuned to life around us, is what mystical traditions have pointed to for millennia as a key doorway to peace and happiness.

Nature's invitation makes this process much easier. We can see how our sense of "self," which seems so solid and real, is really just another aspect of nature that comes and goes, no more real than the thoughts that perpetuate it. The less attention we give it, the more space and ease we feel.

In this practice I invite you to walk outside in nature, away from people. Let yourself meander and be drawn to aspects of the landscape that allure you. As you walk, try to let go of thoughts that pull you from the present and continue to orient to the environment.

Allow attention to absorb into sounds, sights, sensations, colors and light. Notice what happens when you let go of focusing on yourself, your thoughts, and your worries and just attune to what's here. If thoughts surface (which are usually about ourselves), release them and return attention to the nature around you.

Now try lying down and gazing up at the canopy of leaves or clouds floating by in the sky. Let awareness be fully engaged with the visual field so all sense of self drops away, even the idea of someone who is looking. Be present to how seeing happens by itself, just as the poet Li Po describes, and how the "seer" can dissolve. Notice how that feels.

Now close your eyes and let attention drift with the

soundscape. Sometimes when listening to sounds we can feel a sense of our own physical boundary dissolving, softening the divide between inside and outside. There is just sounds arising and being known naturally in awareness.

While listening, see if you can feel the body softening and melting, like it is dissolving into the earth, where the sense of separateness between you and earth diminishes. Let go of any image of the body and just attune to the contact with the ground and any sense of relaxing.

Keep orienting to the sensory world around you, letting go of any ruminating about yourself. Notice what happens as you do this for a longer period of time, perhaps for an hour or even a whole day. Note how that may help soften the sense of self or allow the separation between you and the world to momentarily dissolve. Be mindful of any corresponding well-being or peace that arises when we temporarily forget the "self" and instead are simply present to life.

As you continue to practice in this way, you can come to see that the sense of "self" is itself transient. At times it is very present when self-focused, on our thoughts, worries and problems. And at times it can be quite absent when we are absorbed into the natural world, present to life around us. Once you understand that, you will be able to hold that sense of self with more spaciousness, ease and wisdom, to not be so caught or bothered by its machinations.

CHAPTER FORTY-ONE

OPENING TO DEATH

Earth teach me regeneration, as the seed which rises in spring.

— UTE PRAYER

W hile walking along a favorite beach of mine, I was shocked when I came upon a beached gray whale. It was slowly decomposing, bare ribs exposed, and its flesh was being picked away by vultures. Yet I chose to be present with this majestic being as a way to honor its death and to remind myself of the natural cycle of life.

I have a particular fondness for gray whales as I go watch them with their beautiful young calves every March in Magdalena Bay in Mexico. Seeing this whale dead on the beach was arresting. Yet why should I be shocked? Nature teaches us that the dying process is just a natural part of the circle of life.

Even though contemporary culture and the medical system sees death as a problem or a medical mistake, nature helps us to not see it as an aberration. When we go outdoors, we encounter death and decay everywhere. We can see it in autumn as trees shed leaves. We see it in winter as the cold and frost withers plants and grasses. We can behold it as we see bones, skulls, and shells as we meander along the shore.

As we attune to death in nature, we come to see that it is a natural, even healthy part of the cycle of life. Without winter and the dormant rest period of this season, there could be no spring. Without the decay of leaves in the forest, there would be no nutrients to feed new growth of saplings and trees. Without the march of millions of salmon returning to spawn and give up their lives, there would be no new salmon hatchlings.

Seeing these cycles in nature can help us see the naturalness of our own death. Rather than deny it, we can come into a healthier relationship with our own mortality. It can wake us up to the fragility and preciousness of all life, including those we know and love. Death reminds us not to take anyone or anything for granted.

In this practice, I invite you to take a walk in any natural setting. Pay attention to an aspect of nature that is reflecting this truth of death and decay. Look around on the ground. Notice there is always both regeneration and decay. In grasses, plants and shrubs you will see parts that are flourishing and areas that are decaying or dead.

Similarly, notice the life cycle in trees. In every tree, you will see branches and leaves that are healthy and other limbs that are without life. Notice what happens within you when you observe parts of nature that are rotting or disintegrating. Do you want to look away? Would you rather focus on the beauty and growth?

As you walk, look on the ground for evidence of death.

It may be fallen leaves, dead insects, bones or feathers. Be mindful when you notice these things. Sense what that awareness evokes in you. Is it an attitude of curiosity, compassion, aversion or perhaps indifference?

If it's available, find a dead tree, fallen branch or bones or shells and take some minutes with this experience. If you are with a dead tree, take a seat and simply observe this form. Notice how even in death there is beauty, dignity and presence. A dead tree gives life to many other creatures, from nesting birds to insects. Stay present and sense what this stirs within you.

As you continue this practice, either sitting or walking or both, also call to mind your own mortality. One day too, you will be like these dying or dead beings. The elements of your own body will be recycled and reused and become other life forms. How is it to sense into this reality?

As you bring this practice to a close, see if you can take with you this awareness of death. Notice how bringing awareness of your own mortality and the innate vulnerability of all life can help bring a certain urgency to life, to not taking anything or anyone for granted. It can help you appreciate what *is* here and inspire you to live life more fully.

CHAPTER FORTY-TWO

ENTERING THE MYSTERY

The most beautiful experience we can have is the mysterious. It is the fundamental emotion that stands at the cradle of true art and true science.

— ALBERT EINSTEIN

Life is mysterious. The fact there is life on this rocky earth hurtling through space is a miracle! That cyanobacteria began the wonder of photosynthesis 2.5 billion years ago, harnessing energy from the sun, is a marvel. The fact that they produced the oxygen that then allowed this planet to be habitable for complex life forms billions of years later is itself a revelation.

We are surrounded by mystery. The way a tiny seed blooms into a tomato or apple tree is truly wondrous. Equally unfathomable is how life evolved in miraculous ways—from dragon flies with wings that allow them to fly in all directions, to beetles that can survive in the Sahara by trapping moisture in the air, to bioluminescence that lights up with motion in the seas. In all directions, we are surrounded by the mystery of life.

The miraculous ways life has evolved and adapted to thrive reflects an intelligence we can barely comprehend. When we gaze at the vastness of the night sky with its countless stars shining from space, we are left speechless at the mystery and scale of the cosmos.

In this meditation, I invite you to take a walk out into any natural setting. Begin with calling to mind the attitude of beginner's mind, bringing curiosity in the same way children feel wonder at the tiniest of things. Let your senses open and attention be drawn to what ignites fascination.

Attune to a leaf from a tree, a plant or a blade of grass. Finely attune your attention to the intricacy of this form. Sense how the green chlorophyll of its photosynthesizing cells are able to absorb sunlight and somehow transform that energy into glucose that provides life-giving energy.

Then find a seed, cone, nut or acorn. Reflect on how the intelligence and the D.N.A. of this tiny form can go on to produce a mature maple tree, grasses or plants. Take some moments to sense into the mystery of how life evolves in this way.

As you continue to roam, notice what catches your attention. Perhaps it is the scaly bark of a fir tree and how that crinkly layer allows the tree to protect itself. Attune to flowers and how they are exquisitely designed to lure pollinators with bright colors, fragrance, and pollen, or how they create perfect landing pads for bees and other insects.

Notice how, when you are in nature, everywhere you look there is evidence of mystery. If you encounter a mushroom, notice how it is a sign that mile upon mile of mycelium root structures are threading their way through the soil, giving nutrients and information to countless organisms. And notice how this web allows trees to communicate.

At times, gaze at the ground. Notice how old leaves, plants and twigs are decomposing into the soil, creating nutrients for future life. How miraculous that life supports new life. Nothing is wasted. Reflect on how even in a handful of soil, there are billions of microorganisms there.

Conversely, gaze up at the sky. Notice this thin layer of atmosphere and how that protects life on earth. Observe the mystery of clouds, how moisture from the ocean and evaporating lakes turn into rain and nourish life. A perfect closed-loop cycle.

Keep opening the senses in this way, attuning your attention to whatever evokes a sense of curiosity or wonder. As you orient to mystery, notice what that stirs within. You may marvel at the mystery of being human and how, through your refined senses, you can know this amazing universe and make sense of its colors, forms, sounds, smells and movements.

As you end this practice, try to bring an equally curious attention to what you encounter in your day, whether it is the mystery of using your computer and a different kind of web, to the marvel of another human being, equally complex and mysterious as any other life form on earth!

PART EIGHT
OPENING THE HEART

CHAPTER FORTY-THREE

LOVING THE EARTH

There is nothing in this world that doesn't cease to foster attention and with attention…love. People protect what they love.

— JACQUES-YVES COSTEAU

Every year I lead kayaking meditation retreats in the Sea of Cortez. As part of that experience, I have had the good fortune of being up close with gray whales in Magdalena Bay in Baja Mexico. If we are lucky, as the mother floats close by, a young baby gray whale will swim alongside our small boat and poke its head out of the water. With its deep brown eyes, he or she will gaze at us.

In that moment of priceless eye-gazing, my heart bursts open. It can only be described as love. This interspecies communication between a land-bound creature and an aquatic mammal transcends separation. It is in these times that I feel my heart bloom with love and a care for life that knows no bounds.

It's the same heart opening I feel when I see a newborn

fawn lying vulnerably in a meadow, or swallow chicks shivering in their nests waiting for their parents to feed them. The heart can be easily moved in many ways—to love spontaneously the majesty of an old-growth redwood, to feel compassion for the tenderness of a desert tortoise hiding in its shell, to experience radiant joy watching starlings murmurate in the sky.

In this meditation, you are invited to explore the heart and the ways that it loves the natural world. For this practice, take a walk outdoors in a place that touches your heart. It may be to a favorite place in nature, a beloved grove of trees, a cherished part of your garden, a pretty park or beside an enchanted stream.

Then take a seat or comfortable posture and absorb your senses into this place. Let your eyes take in what you appreciate. Notice what you feel fond of. As you do this, sense your heart and how it feels in relation to each thing you feel drawn to.

Then tune into greater detail and specificity. If you are with a tree, notice all her contours, her skin-like bark, her silent presence, the dappled light of her leaves. If gazing at a bird, notice his colorful plumage, his alertness, and the particular way he flies. Observe any response in your heart. Is there a tenderness, affection or love for this beautiful form?

Notice each of your senses and how they can be portals to your loving heart. As you listen to the enchanting birdsong, be curious if that evokes a heartfelt fondness. Touching the silkiness of a flower petal, or the delicateness of moist moss, sense if that kindles affection or care.

Continue to practice in this way, either while seated or while walking. Then pause each time something touches your heart—the flight of a butterfly, the tenacity of a dung beetle walking on the ground, the scent of jasmine or ponderosa bark. Take this experience in and notice any quality of love that may be evoked.

With each passing experience, you can also extend love from your heart through wishing these life forms well. Standing by an old oak, you can wish it to be well-nourished. Seeing a young animal, you may wish it to be safe. Listening to the sounds of a stream, you may wish for it to be protected. Seeing a flock of acorn woodpeckers playing, you may wish them to be happy together.

In this way, you are not just feeling love or care, but actively expressing your heart's wish for life around you. You can do this silently, or you may whisper these wishes quietly to the ferns, frogs and flowers. Observe what happens in your heart when you radiate this love to the natural world around you. Notice if it brings a sense of kinship or deeper connection.

Continue to practice in this way for as long as feels engaging. Know that you can draw forth this quality of love by simply attuning to the present moment and sensing the heart's relationship to the natural world around you.

CHAPTER FORTY-FOUR

SENSING LOVE FROM NATURE

Such love does the sky pour out, that whenever I stand in a field, when I get home, I have to wring out my clothes.

— ST. FRANCIS OF ASSISI

As we become more attuned and sensitive to the natural world, what becomes more apparent is the love we can feel from nature. We can begin to tune into the benevolence of natural landscapes. We sense a welcoming attitude and complete absence of judgment. We can observe a quality of total acceptance, where every being is welcome, accepted and cared for just as they are.

This is so different from the human world, where we are so often riddled with our own self-judgment or feel criticism, rejection or indifference from individuals or groups.

The earth is inherently generous, offering its abundance to all. Just think of all the ways you are lovingly cared for without being asked anything in return. We are fed with bountiful food from the earth and oceans. We are hydrated with rains and waters. Our lungs fill with clean, fresh oxygen produced by trees. The sun warms our body and the dark of the night allows us to sleep. All of this is given freely, and you could say, lovingly.

As I write, I sit amidst a new-growth redwood forest. The trees stand still, patient and grounded. They exude a warmth and kind presence. They whisper wordlessly, "welcome, you are home here, stay awhile and drink from this quiet sanctuary." Sometimes students share how trees invite them to offload their grief and shed their tears. It's as if they wrap their branches around us, comforting our heavy hearts.

In this meditation, try to go into a natural setting where you feel immersed in nature, perhaps a forest or woodland, somewhere you can feel held or cocooned by the natural world. As you walk around, open your senses, feel the pores of your skin open, and try to shift into a state of receptivity, where you feel the impression of the landscape.

You can continue to walk or if you feel drawn to a particular place, take a seat, lie down or lean against a tree and attune your attention to what is present here. Notice if you feel any sense of welcoming from the trees, grasses, plants, birds or other creatures. Can you notice a sense of invitation, of welcoming you here?

Look specifically at the trees. Feel their presence. Sense how they and other beings in the environment are aware of your presence through smell, touch, sound, energy or otherwise. Notice if you feel any warmth, love or benevolence exuding from the trees. It may be quite subtle. Maybe you note it by sensing how relaxed, calm, quiet or safe you feel. Perhaps it is a quality of being held by them, or maybe you feel directly their loving energy.

If your rational, critical mind tries to doubt or question any of this, notice that and invite the mind to relax, to soften and for a while to step aside. Continue to sense your heart, your body and the environment. Observe how everything natural offers itself. Not to you specifically, but shares itself with life all around. Sense this natural abundance and generosity of spirit in every living thing.

Now shift your attention to something small and particular, like a flower, a blade of grass, a ladybug. Can you sense how love may be the generating principle behind each life form, each expression of life? If you can sense a flavor or aspect of love coming from nature, observe how you experience it in this moment. Sense how it affects your heart or influences your body. How does it touch your mind?

In this way, as you sit, lie down, walk or rest, continue to attune to the love that you may feel emanating from nature. Feel into how we can receive this transmission of love in any moment. It is always here, we just mostly don't attune to it, and so miss what a loving and benevolent environment we live in.

As you end this practice, notice if there is any reciprocal quality of love, care or gratitude that emerges within you towards the kindness that is offered to us in nature. Let any appreciation flow towards the landscape you are in. Notice how this may bring a natural sense of care and desire to protect this precious earth and this particular place, ecosystem or being. By doing so we complete the cycle of love.

CHAPTER FORTY-FIVE

CULTIVATING GRATITUDE

Nature's beauty is a gift that cultivates appreciation and gratitude.

— LOUIE SCHWARTZBERG

R obin Wall Kimmerer, a member of the Citizen Potawatomi Nation, writes that her elders say the earth asks of us two important things: to pay attention and to offer gratitude. How different would our lives be if we took this advice to heart and lived by it?

When we feel and offer gratitude, we shift from a scarcity mindset of never feeling we have enough, to realizing how much we all have and are given by this abundant and generous earth. When we reflect on what we appreciate and what we can give thanks for, we quickly realize it ties us into every part of this earth and all beings who live here.

I've had a gratitude practice for decades. It is one of my favorite practices because it instantly shifts my mood, perspective and well-being. It's hard to feel grateful and stay grumpy! I particularly enjoy stretching what it is I'm appreciative of. So I remember to give thanks to the sewage workers, road crews and plumbers that keep our infrastructure going. I also take a bow to all the pollinating insects who pollinate and allow us to eat!

In this practice, the focus is to attune to what you may be feeling grateful for in nature and why you have such gratitude. So head outdoors into a place that you love to explore. Once you arrive at a suitable place, take a seat and settle in.

Take a moment to look around you and begin to attune to all the life that's here. Notice any natural quality of appreciation that may come for what is around you. And as you turn your attention to each particular part of the landscape here—leaves, trees, grasses, flowers, insects, birds, stones and hills—notice if you feel grateful for their presence.

When gratitude touches you, sense how that feels. It can often be sensed as a warm, soft glow in the heart or body. It can feel expansive. Most importantly it can allow us to connect with the experience we are grateful for and to feel a sense of warmth, connection and care for it.

As you sense into each thing in your environment, pause when you are grateful for something and ask yourself why you feel grateful for that particular thing, whether it be a leaf, rock or tree. When we understand why we are grateful, it significantly enhances the meaning and power of that experience of gratitude.

For example, to know that I'm grateful for trees for the life-giving oxygen they exhale, for their ability to embody presence and stillness, and for their beauty and their majesty, allows me to enrich that experience of grate-fulness.

Continue to sense what you have gratitude for. It may come in the form of sounds, like birdsong. Or it may come to you as a sensation, like breeze, wind or rain. It may appear as a fragrance. Or it may just be a general love and appreciation for the landscape, forest or park.

Whatever comes, continue to sense into this quality of gratefulness, for the gift of life. You may also feel grateful for your body and senses that allow you to know this magical earth in which we live.

Finally, you may also reflect on all the people who support you in this moment and in the past, people who have encouraged you to meditate or connect with nature. What happens in your heart when you recollect them?

In this way, we come to feel gratitude for the whole circle of life and remember that we are intimately supported in all moments by a myriad of life forms. And gratitude is the healthiest response to that. When we feel grateful, we are most likely to reciprocate that emotion with care and responsive action, to protect that which we are grateful for.

PART NINE
MEDITATING INDOORS

CHAPTER FORTY-SIX

MEDITATING WITH A PLANT

Flowers always make people better, happier, and more helpful; they are sunshine, food and medicine for the soul.

— LUTHER BURBANK

Nature Meditation can be done anywhere. It can be cultivated in a wild desert landscape, atop a rugged mountain or in a city park. It can be equally developed in your home garden and even indoors with a houseplant or gazing at a tree from a window.

In these practices, the quality of presence one brings to the natural world matters more than how spectacular the environment is. Grand landscapes can evoke feelings of awe and the sacred, but we can also access qualities of joy and peace in the simplest things. We can experience these as a butterfly lands on a nearby fence, or a hummingbird feeds by our kitchen window.

In this meditation, sit by a plant, flower, succulent or

cacti. If no flora is present in the house then you can also gaze at a tree or plant through a window.

Take some moments as you begin sitting to close your eyes and cultivate mindful attention to your physical experience. Sense your posture and any physical sensations that are present. Allow awareness to permeate your breath. Sit quietly breathing and sensing for a few minutes, releasing thoughts that pull you away from here.

Then open your eyes and take in the plant in front of you. Let go of any labels about what kind of plant or flower it is and shift instead to your immediate experience of it. Absorb attention into the form of the plant. Notice all the stems, leaves, buds and flowers. Observe where it is thriving and where it is decaying.

Be mindful how light illuminates it. See how light penetrates through the leaves and flowers. Notice the rich variety of color and all the shades of green and other hues. Be curious what draws you in the visual field. Sense what gazing at this living being evokes in you.

Now explore the plant through touch. You may close your eyes and allow the fingers to gently and carefully examine its leaves, stem, petals, stamens, roots. Sense the textures, smoothness, roughness and other sensations. Be mindful how mindful touch informs you about this plant.

Observe if the plant has any fragrance. Notice if the stem, leaves or flower have varying scents. Try rubbing a leaf or petal and see if that releases any smell.

Then take in this plant with all your senses, with an open receptive attention. Be curious what being with this plant, tree or flower evokes in you. Notice if there is a deepening connection, affection or love, or any other emotion as you do this practice.

Stay open to sensing something beyond the physical form of this plant. It may be a presence, energy, or stillness. You may attune to mystery, knowing this plant emerges from a seed or bulb. Perhaps you connect with its ancient intelligence and its adaptive resilience. Or you may intuit a quality of the sacred, as each living thing connects us to something vast and unknowable.

Continue to practice in this way. If you feel drawn you can then extend this way of being with other natural elements in your environment indoors, in your garden or on a balcony. Notice how even the smallest thing, from a bumble bee that accidentally flies into your home or a spider weaving a web in the eaves of your house, can tune us to nature's wonders.

CHAPTER FORTY-SEVEN

GAZING THROUGH A WINDOW

A morning-glory at my window satisfies me more than the meta-physics of books.

— WALT WHITMAN

There are many times we are drawn to connecting with nature, but are unable to do so. Freezing temperatures, howling winds and torrential rains may deter us from venturing outdoors. Physical injury or limitations can restrict outdoor movements. Limited access to natural areas in a sprawling city may also be prohibitive.

Yet there is rarely a time where we can't look out a window and see something natural. Even if it is just a slice of sky, a lone tree on the street, a patch of grass or rain pouring down from clouds above. It can be surprising how impactful a humble vista of nature can be.

In this meditation, sit by a window where you can see various aspects of nature. Find a comfortable chair and sit upright yet relaxed. For a few minutes, close your eyes and be present to the physical sensations of sitting and breathing, orienting awareness to this sensory moment.

Once you feel grounded and present, slowly open your eyes and lower your gaze. Be aware that you are mindfully seeing. Try to soften the gaze and relax the eyes to invite a quality of receptivity. Then look out the window and let your eyes roam across this particular vista. Be curious about what draws you in the visual field.

Rather than darting around with your eyes, let them settle onto one thing. It may be a tree, fields, clouds or plants. Steady your gaze here and fully take in this experience. Bring a beginner's mind to this experience as if seeing it for the first time. What can you observe? What can you know of its shape, light, color, form and movement? How is it in relationship with everything else in its environment?

Notice what you observe subtly change with sunlight and shade, with wind and rain, in movement and stillness. Reflect how this visual experience differs at dawn, midday and dusk. Be mindful of what looking outside in this way evokes in you. Each part of nature is capable of inspiring curiosity, delight, reflection, pleasure or displeasure and other reactions.

Now open up your gaze and look around until something else catches your attention. Repeat the same process of studying a part of nature, which could be a shrub, a lawn, an animal, or the setting sun. Let the eyes settle to fully take this experience in. Let go of thinking about what you see and instead receive its texture and hue, its movements and shape. What can you discover anew?

Beyond the particular features in the environment you may study, notice if you "sense" any qualities nature transmits, even from the comfort of being indoors. You may feel a sense of presence of the old trees you gaze at. Raptors and vultures may evoke a sense of raw wildness. A hummingbird may inspire delight. Gazing at clouds may instill a sense of softness and ease.

Continue to gaze in this way for some time. Be curious about the relationship between the world "outside" and your inner landscape of heart and mind. Sense how the natural world often evokes qualities and feelings within us. Just by gazing out a window into nature, you can realize you are part of something much larger, a broader ecosystem that you are innately part of and always connected to.

As you end this practice, be mindful of the impact of this simple meditation. Know that it is available from every window of your life, from your house, office or car!

PART TEN
MEDITATING WITH THE FOUR SEASONS

CHAPTER FORTY-EIGHT
MEDITATING IN SPRING— EMERGENCE AND POSSIBILITY

It is spring again. The earth is like a child that knows poems by heart.

— RAINER MARIA RILKE

How wonderful that with each revolution of the earth around the sun, we experience four different seasons, each with their distinctive gifts. And none are perhaps more beautiful than spring. It is hard not to feel excitement and a sense of possibility as life emerges from the darker, colder, dormant time of winter. It is a season of joy.

In spring, life bursts forth from the earth. Buds come into blossom. Crocus, snowdrops and daffodils emerge from hardened soil. Myriad shades of green once again adorn the forest canopy and fields are laden with emerald grasses. Newborn lambs frolic in meadows while birds returning from winter migrations sing heartily from treetops.

It is a fecund season, where spring can also bloom within our own heart and inspire feelings of excitement, delight and hope. Newfound energy can emerge within us, ready to begin new endeavors. It is a time to remember the tenacity of life emerging from the slumber of winter and to rejoice in beauty offered from wildflowers and morning song.

In this meditation, take a walk into a favorite natural setting where there is plenty of evidence of the blossoming spring. As you walk, turn your attention to signs of new life, being aware of what you behold around you and if that stirs anything within your own body and heart.

Take in the fresh green grasses that carpet the ground. Notice the blossoms and the variety of wildflowers. Let your eyes soak up the new leaves, some perhaps still tightly coiled, some bursting open. Observe how bright many leaves are as they first unfold. What other signs of life do you see? How does such beauty gladden your heart?

Attend to the new life that you can see on the branches of trees. Notice how evergreen trees are creating new growth of fresh emerald needles on the tips of their limbs. It speaks to the fecundity of life ever prepared to extend itself forward.

Remember to also absorb spring's goodness through your nose. So much fragrance is released as flowers emerge to attract pollinators, as the season promotes a burst of fertility. Be sure to get close to blossoms and flowers to inhale their scents.

When you come across a place, perhaps a meadow, some wildflowers, fresh grasses, or a tree in bud or blossom, take a moment to pause, to sit and meditate there and drink in this experience more fully.

Let your attention absorb these particular expressions of emergence, particularly plants and grasses emerging from the soil. See the tender shoots that have barely broken ground. Then close your eyes and sense what stirs within you as you take this fresh life in. Does it evoke any emotion? Perhaps it inspires a sense of possibility as you feel the tenacity of life.

Similarly, observe the sounds, listening with full awareness to the soundscape. Spring is a time when birds return from migration and begin establishing their territory and nests. Listen to the males sing heartily from branches and treetops. Notice the differing birdsong that is present now. Sense how uplifting their sweet song can be. Let that joyfulness soak into your own being.

Lastly, as you take in spring's abundance, notice how spring is equally emerging within you. What may want to grow forth from winter's slumber? What possibility is waking up within as you feel the emergence of life all around? How is that newfound energy wishing to express itself? As you sense life regenerating, is there anything wanting to regenerate in your own life?

As you end the meditation, remember to keep taking in the fullness of spring as you go outdoors and receive the beauty and bounty of this beautiful season. Let the joy bring solace to your heart.

CHAPTER FORTY-NINE
MEDITATING IN SUMMER ON ABUNDANCE

It was June, and the world smelled of roses. The sunshine was like powdered gold over the grassy hillside.

— MAUD HART LOVELACE

I, like many, remember fondly the summers of my childhood. In that precious season, the long, light-filled days were spent bathing in the sun, swimming in streams, walking through lush forests teeming with life. I recall warm, balmy nights listening to the sounds of cicadas. Summer days felt spacious and the lighter nights provided a luxury of time.

In one of my favorite memories, I'm lying in a field of golden wheat in late summer, tall stalks swaying in the breeze set against an infinite blue sky, flies buzzing overhead, swallows swooping in the air, grasshoppers clicking. The whole ambience exuded a sense of deep ease. It reminds me of a phrase from the writer Sam Keen, "Deep summer is when laziness finds respectability."

Of course, summer evokes different things for all of us. Yet childhood recollections often point to the qualities of this season—warming, nourishing and playful. It is the earth's celebration of life at its peak growth and fullness. And it can evoke for us a sense of abundance, relaxation, pleasure and fun.

In this meditation, go out on a warm summer's day. Take a walk into one of your cherished landscapes. It may be to walk along farmers' fields. Or perhaps in a lush city park or out into rolling hills and meadows or in a vibrant forest. Wherever you roam, go to a place that expresses the fullness of summer.

As you walk, sense into the particular quality of this season. Notice the vibrancy of color and the fecundity of life as you take in the earth's abundance. Observe how verdant the ground is, how it teems with life, with plants and grasses moving into every ecological niche. Take in the display of summer's opulence in its rich flowers and leaves. Be curious what qualities this evokes in you.

Then take a seat in a place that draws you, where it is easy to continue to sense into this summer-y landscape. As you sit and close your eyes, feel the warmth that comes in summer, that warms the air and allows your body to soften and open. Notice how just the temperature can invite a quality of relaxation and ease.

Now open your attention to the soundscape here. Are there sounds that are distinct to this season? Listen to the crickets, grasshoppers or cicadas that are more pronounced in summer, that for many are evocative of this season. What birdsong is here at this time? What else calls your attention in this soundscape?

Similarly, as you breathe, sense into the particular

smells here. Perhaps you can sense the rich summer fragrance of grasses or freshly mown lawns. Is the air perfumed with fragrance from flowers?

Continue to open your senses in this way, noticing how your body and heart are influenced by all the impressions of this season. As you feel into summer's impact, reflect what this time of year evokes for you. Is there anything the natural world is inviting in you or into your life? Perhaps it may be an invitation to slow down, or to enjoy the earth's bounty, or to play and delight in the sensory world and to appreciate its beauty and abundance.

CHAPTER FIFTY

MEDITATING IN AUTUMN— FULLNESS AND LETTING GO

If you want a little peace, let go a little. If you want a lot of peace let go a lot. If you want complete peace, let go completely.

— ACHAAN CHAH

Autumn is an exquisite season, one that has so many gifts. The light of the sun is softer, casting long shadows across the earth. Fruits are heavy on the boughs of trees. The turning colors of the leaves cloak the forest in rich golds and crimson.

And for many, it is a time of reflection. It is a poignant time where we leave the exuberance of summer and head into a more melancholic season, tinged with a sadness for the loss of that fullness, where life begins its slow release into the fallow winter. It invites us to slow down, to pause, to gather the harvest both from the land but also from within.

The once-blooming plants and the lush green canopy begin to brown and wilt. Leaves slowly shed from branches and bushes. As we watch the autumnal winds strip the trees of their canopy, we are reminded of the ways trees let go, releasing their leaves to the air, their fruit to the ground, to become food for the forest and compost for new life.

And in this time, we may reflect for ourselves of what we need to shed, of where we are being asked to release, to not hold on, to let go to the winds that blow through our life, to live more lightly in this world, to be prepared for the next season, the next chapter in our journey.

In this meditation, take a walk into a forest, a woodland or out into dried meadows or harvested farmland where the presence of autumn is evident. Meander in the forest or among trees, where you can see the verdant canopy turning golden, crimson and brown. Look at the plants in the ground and see how their colors are also slowly turning, their leaves and stems wilting, drying, heading slowly toward the earth.

As you stroll, take in the sights of autumn, sense into the quality of this season of release as you see leaves falling to earth. What does it evoke within you? Notice the mood that autumn can bring. Is it one of melancholy, joy or sadness? Sometimes, for some, there can be resistance to the presence of autumn as it brings the knowledge of the cold and darker winter ahead. Be open to whatever quality is present now.

After walking a while, find somewhere to sit where you can take in the presence of the autumnal landscape. Notice the colors around you and all the signs of life slowing down that the autumn can reveal. Perhaps you can sense the quality of restfulness that is present after the industriousness of spring and summer. Or maybe there is still the full-ness of autumn as you see the fruits on trees.

Then close your eyes and feel into what quality is present in your body. Feel your legs on the ground, in the same ways leaves begin to rest on the earth. How does your body feel in response to autumn? Perhaps there is a quality of ease or softness that is reflecting something similar in the environment.

And as the cold and the wind begins to remind the trees that it is their turn to release their summer coat of leaves, you may feel a similar invitation. What is being asked of you to shed, to release, to let go of what no longer serves you? Perhaps habits, patterns and activities that interfere with well-being? What burden are you being invited to put down?

Hold these questions and reflections lightly, but continue to inquire as to what this autumnal season evokes for you and what gifts letting go may bring in your life. You may wish to journal if any insights come about this poignant time.

CHAPTER FIFTY-ONE

MEDITATING IN WINTER— ON FALLOWNESS AND REST

Sometimes you need the fields to lie fallow in order to gain nutrients.

— CHEECH MARIN

I n days of old, winters were a blessed time of rest. The earth lays fallow, often frozen, muddy or blanketed in snow. Work on the land was minimal. And when we lived according to the rhythms of the sun, as the winter nights drew short, we would sleep earlier and longer. Our rhythm mirrored the cycle of nature, which slows down and becomes dormant.

Every natural cycle has periods of growth, abundance, decay and death. The earth and her seasons express just that. Our life also moves to the same rhythms. Yet we live in a culture that prioritizes spring and summer, celebrates growth, productivity and high yields. We have mostly forgotten how to slow down or to rest. We seldom allow for fallow periods, necessary for the body and heart to replenish, to be ready for the next season of activity.

Yet winter provides a beautiful opportunity to do just that. Fresh snow on the ground hushes all sound into quietude, inducing a tranquility into the landscape. Falling rain invites us to gaze peacefully at the replenishing waters. Frozen lakes and ponds remind us to be still, to rest in place.

In this meditation, you may choose to do this outdoors if the elements allow. Or you can do this looking through a window at a natural landscape at a time when winter's weather is unleashing its gifts.

Begin by walking outdoors if you can, even if it is raining or snowing (just wear suitable clothing). Pay attention to how the landscape reflects the season. Notice the ground and whether it is frozen, hard or muddy from the rains. Observe the flora and how plants have withered into the soil. Be mindful of bare trees, silhouetted stark against the sky.

If comfortable, take a seat, perhaps on a stump, fallen tree or rock. Bring awareness to all your senses. Feel the coldness of the air and how it feels against your exposed skin. It is possible to stay relaxed even though there can be a natural contraction against the cold. Notice if there is an invigorating quality to the air as you inhale.

Attune to the stillness that is often so present in winter. Observe how little life stirs, how quietly the trees stand, frozen in place. Be mindful of the absence of birdsong or insect life. What do you feel as you sense that?

If you are out on a snowy day, take in that serenity of falling snow and the beautiful way it dusts the landscape white. Attune to the beautiful quietude that snow brings and the way it can make even the ugliest thing sparkle. Observe how silent everything is and the way it hushes all sound. Notice what the stillness evokes within you and whether it supports an inner quietude.

If you are walking in the rain or standing under a tree as rain falls, give that experience your full attention. Notice the sounds of the rain on leaves, on your clothing, as it splashes the ground. What quality is evoked as you gaze at the rain falling from the heavens, replenishing the earth?

As you continue to sense the wintery landscape, how does being outside at this time of year influence your mind, body and heart? Be curious if the quietude of the landscape, the fallowness of farmers' fields and the frozen ground impacts you in any way. Does it invite within you a similar desire to be quiet or fallow? Does the restfulness of this season evoke the desire to rest more in your own life?

Continue to meditate and reflect in this way, either sitting down or, if too cold, then walking or standing. Keep opening to the gifts of this season and the lessons therein.

PART ELEVEN
QUESTIONING DEEPLY

CHAPTER FIFTY-TWO

MEDITATING WITH THE ECO-CRISIS

We don't inherit the earth from our ancestors, we borrow it from our children.

— DAVID BROWER

To open our hearts and minds to nature these days is no easy thing. If you have come this far in the book, you already have a deep love and care for the earth. And you are also aware of the tragedy that befalls every living ecosystem on the planet and every species struggling to survive.

To be aware in nature is to feel what Australian eco-psychologist Glenn Albrecht calls "solostalgia," which is to feel simultaneously grief and sadness at what is happening to the places in nature we love. We grieve because we love and our heart breaks at times when we hear about the loss of species or the degradations of coral reefs, oceans, soil, forests and rivers.

Yet, we also know that closing our hearts in fear, hatred

or anger does not help. It only compounds our pain. Mindfulness in nature is courageous in that it encourages us to stay aware of what is happening, to not turn away, to feel what comes up in response to the ecological crisis.

In this meditation, you will turn your attention to the natural world, but also to the emotions and pain that may surface when you sense directly or reflect on the harm being done to species and the living systems of the earth.

Go outdoors to a place of natural beauty. It may be a place that is thriving. And it may also be an area where signs of the ecological crisis are evident. Begin by walking around and soaking in the natural beauty of this place. Drink in the colors, sounds, forms, and other features that allure your attention.

Then take a seat where you can see or sense something that reflects the challenges facing this ecosystem. It may be near trees that are stressed due to lack of rain. Or it may be in a woodland that is subject to beetle infestation or disease, which is reflective of a changing climate. It may be looking at parched ground, or dried up creeks, streams or a shrunken reservoir.

If there is nothing obviously reflecting environmental challenges, then you can call to mind species or areas that you know about or have seen that are negatively impacted.

Begin the practice by closing your eyes, and sense your body as part of the earth, sitting on its surface. Sense your breath, breathing with trees and grasses and animals. Then open your eyes at something that expresses climate distress. Or simply call to mind what is challenged in your region, perhaps the ocean, or forests, or a watershed.

Notice how you feel as you take in this parched forest or struggling watershed. What happens when you call to mind endangered species struggling to survive? Sense your heart, perhaps putting a hand on your chest and feeling your breath there as a way to connect to the emotions present.

Make space for whatever emotions surface. There may be a mix of feelings, like sadness, grief, loss or sorrow. The climate crisis may evoke anger, rage and indignation. Not uncommonly it can trigger numbness, a not wanting to feel, a desire to turn away. Sometimes it creates a sense of overwhelm, helplessness and despair. Often it stirs anxiety and fear of what our lives and our children's lives may become.

Whatever arises, keep breathing with the feelings that surface. If thoughts, judgments or plans arise, try to release them and return to sensing your body, heart and feelings. Know that the feelings are a reflection of your love. And remember that even the strongest of feelings are waves that ebb and flow.

If the emotions are too strong, open your eyes and look at something that brings pleasure or ease. Do this until you feel more balanced and centered. You may also need to get up, walk around and continue to take in the beauty and goodness of the landscape you are in until you feel more grounded and less overwhelmed.

After a period of time of sensing your heart's response to the ecological crisis, observe what may want to emerge from this practice. Perhaps a desire to engage in some action, or to reach out to friends and colleagues to discuss your responses. Or there may simply be the commitment to not turn from the pain of the reality of the ecological crisis and allow that to inform you, your life and your decisions.

CHAPTER FIFTY-THREE

REFLECTING ON HOW THE EARTH WISHES TO MOVE THROUGH YOU
ADDITIONAL MEDITATION

Live the questions now, and gradually far in the future, without even noticing it, you will gradually live your way into the answer.

— RAINER MARIA RILKE

After you have spent time in nature with these contemplative meditations, you will have a more intimate relationship with the species of birds, trees and other flora and fauna where you live. Your body, heart and mind will be opened by these nature-based practices.

As you meditate outdoors, questions may arise about how this deeper relationship with the earth can inform your life, its direction, and decisions you make. It may inspire you to live a life more in harmony with nature, more aligned with living simply, more regenerative for the earth and species.

In this meditation, we will explore such contemplations. Begin by going out to a favorite local nature setting. That may be your garden, a park, beside a particular tree, stream or in a woodland. Take some time to settle into meditation in this familiar place. Open your senses to the sounds, sights, smells and ambience here. Notice all the flora and fauna that abound around you.

Then settle your attention inward and for some minutes focus on the simplicity of breath, remembering you are breathing with all life and all photosynthesizing flora.

With an awareness of the connection of your inner and outer world, when your mind is quieter, ask this question, "How does the earth wish to move through me?" With this kind of contemplative inquiry, simply ask this question, and then let it settle, in the same way a stone thrown in a pond settles slowly to the ground.

Let the question permeate your body so it is a full-bodied inquiry. Don't necessarily look for an answer right away. You don't need to settle for the first thing that comes to mind. Let it be a slow percolating, a metabolizing of the question and concern, "How does the earth wish to move through me?"

It may be an answer that comes not from within you but from the trees, birds or the soil under you. Perhaps the stones have something to say about the matter. Maybe the sun warming you is what speaks. Or perhaps nothing comes but a quiet resolve to ensure that your life is lived in a way that is in harmony with the earth, so you live lightly and carefully on this planet.

Continue to hold the question in your heart and listen carefully to what may arise for you. The answer may be very clear. You may already be living in a way that perfectly expresses how the earth wishes to move through you. Or perhaps you are not living in alignment and deep in your bones you sense there is a different way that you could be living, working, or acting that more fully expresses your love of the earth and the beings who live here.

Sometimes sitting is a good way to explore this question. But for some, perhaps lying on the earth is a better posture. For others it may be better to stroll, to meander while holding the inquiry and seeing what comes to you that way. Mindful walking can be a very supportive way to have wise thoughts move through you.

You may decide to take a whole day with this inquiry. Or you may choose to open this discussion with others and see what comes when you have a reflective conversation with people who also share this same question or concern.

Whatever comes, take time to let any wisdom in. Then write it down in a journal and further clarify it. Once it has become clear, share it with people who will understand your intention and inquiry. Then let this clarity guide how you live, move and act in this world. The earth is waiting for all of us to live with more alignment, to wake up to the beauty of this earth and to live in harmony with it and to protect all of the beautiful life forms that call this home.

ABOUT THE AUTHOR
MARK COLEMAN

MARK COLEMAN is a renowned meditation teacher. He is a senior teacher at Spirit Rock Meditation Center in Marin County, CA, and has led insight meditation retreats worldwide for over twenty years. Mark has studied meditation since 1981, primarily within the Buddhist tradition. Trained by Jack Kornfield and others, Mark is also influenced by Advaita Vedanta teachings, Dzogchen practice and the Diamond Approach school.

Through his organization, Awake in the Wild, Mark helps others explore the integration of meditation and the natural world. From Alaska to Peru, he guides nature-based meditation retreats based on his book, *Awake in the Wild: Mindfulness in Nature as a Path of Self-Discovery*. Mark also facilitates yearlong nature meditation teacher trainings to help others spread the work of nature-based mindfulness.

Mark is co-founder of The Mindfulness Training Institute, which trains mindfulness teachers in the US and Europe annually. He is the author of three books on mindfulness: *From Suffering to Peace: The True Promise of Mindfulness, Awake in the Wild: Mindfulness in Nature as a Path to Self-Discovery,* and *Make Peace With Your Mind: How Mindfulness and Compassion Can Help Free You from the Inner Critic.*

Mark is a leader in developing mindfulness programs and has created programs for companies like British Airways and The New York Times, and for apps including Insight Timer, Mindfulness, Whil, Muse and others. He is also an expert in mindfulness consulting and has worked internationally with corporations, non-profit organizations, governments and the United Nations.

Originally from Northern England, Mark now lives in Northern California and likes nothing more than spending his free time hiking, biking, kayaking and backpacking in the mountains.

To learn more about Mark's work and Awake in the Wild, visit:

https://markcoleman.org/
https://www.awakeinthewild.com/

Printed in Great Britain
by Amazon

42245877R00128